CW00521766

# A Trav~~e~~ ~~.~~ ~~..~~ ~~g...~~

How did it all start for me?

I was born in September 1941, just a year after the Battle of Britain, and grew up during the austerity of post-war Britain. For my family, and countless other middle class families, 'holidays' meant the annual fortnight in a British seaside resort: Clacton-on-Sea, Bognor Regis, Bournemouth, Torquay and so on. What memories they hold!

My secondary school, Latymer Upper, in Hammersmith, West London, had been a pioneer in setting up exchange arrangements with the Johanneum, the oldest school in Hamburg, from as early as 1948, when the city was still in ruins, and with the Lycee Chaptal in Paris. But I was too timid to take advantage of these opportunities, probably because of dreadful memories of being sent by my well-meaning father on a Wolf Cubs' camp run by his Office Secretary in the 1950s. I was so homesick then that my poor father had to come down to Sussex to rescue me from Akela and her tribe. It was a very awkward journey home with him on the Southern Railway!

During the post-war years Britons venturing abroad were subject to a Foreign Currency Allowance. As late as 1969 this was still limited to £60 per person. I well remember seeing, in an upmarket travel agent's window in St James', a beautiful model of the former Royal Mail Line's flagship *Andes* with a banner across it proclaiming the good news (for those who could afford it) that *'Andes* IS Sterling Area!'

The era of mass package tours was still a long way off, to say nothing of today's huge Butlins-type cruise ships, so I felt myself privileged, in that my first trip abroad was in 1962. I had been given a grant from my wealthy and generous Oxford college, St John's, to venture to the South of France with a young people's group organized by the legendary pioneering travel agent, Miss Erna Low.

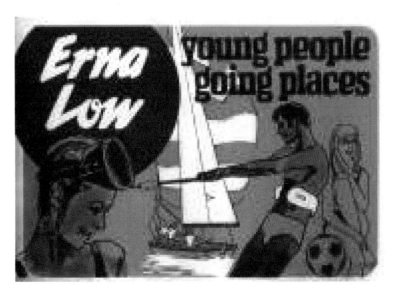

*Erna Low's Young People's Travel Brochure 1960s*

I had gone up to St John's in 1960 to read Modern History and our benevolent college President, Dr William Conrad Costin, announced a year or two later that he was shocked to discover some undergraduates had *actually been taking jobs* during the Long Vacation! Like many other students I had a useful holiday job on the sales staff of Harrods store, which I enjoyed so much that for a while I contemplated making a career in retail, after I'd taken my degree. But I failed Harrods' intelligence test! It was something to do with matching up buttons..... Returning to college life, Costin's traditional view was that the Long Vac "was intended for

# THOSE WERE THE WAVES!

## The Heyday of Cruising Recalled

### RICHARD MARTIN

Oxford 2020

*The Author, Grand Canal, Venice 1990s*

ISBN No: 9798656134897

# Preface

Facing enforced cancellation of cruises during the Covid-19 lockdown and consequent unexpected leisure at home, my thoughts have turned to the past half century or more of cruise lecturing that I have enjoyed, mostly through luck and good fortune. It struck me that others might like to share some of my memories of a vanished world, as we await news of future cruises and wonder how the industry will be able to go forward in these testing times.

At Easter I received an invitation from the excellent Catholic seafarers' charity Stella Maris, celebrating its hundredth year of support for seafarers, to share my memories: another stimulus to writing them at this time of enforced seclusion!

Having grown up during the Second World War and its long aftermath, which lasted well into the 1950s in Britain, I am apprehensive about the length of the Emergency and its aftermath, particularly in regard to our ability to travel freely. As I look back it seems I have been incredibly lucky in experiencing what may turn out to have been the Golden Age of Cruising.

Finally, I would like to express my thanks to my old friend Brian Joplin for his unfailing encouragement and helpful suggestions and to the many shipping lines whose guest lecturer I have had the privilege of being over the years.

reading and travel" and that anyone in need of finance to travel should apply to the College. The President, as you may gather, was a bachelor don of the old school! When his time came to retire from a life spent entirely within the college, except for the little matter of distinguished service in the First World War, he declared, "I never married. I married the College," to thunderous cheers from the assembled body! I recall his old-fashioned outrage at the idea of vacation jobs actually got into the papers! Anyway, it was too good to miss and I speedily took up his kind offer of a travel grant. He had clearly forgotten a sticky interview I had with him at the end of my first year, when my tutors had read out their rather scathing reports of my progress at the end of term Collections meeting. On that occasion Costin had exclaimed, "Well, Martin, we took you on the expectation that you would contribute to College life, but this is ridiculous!"

Whether the President had envisaged a grant for a young person's party to the French Riviera, rather than an earnest trip to view Greek ruins, was irrelevant, since the college never required any report of how one had spent the travel grant! If pressed, I would have pointed, somewhat lamely, to the fact that I was studying 'The Making of the Anglo-French Entente' as my Special Subject in the History School.

Our accommodation on the French Riviera, a youth hostel midway between old Antibes and smart Juan les Pins, was somewhat primitive. A large open hut-dormitory for the boys, while the girls were accommodated in the old house. But that first visit stirred my love for France and the Mediterranean, after some initial shocks, like the hole-in-the-floor lavatories, which took me quite a while to work out how to use correctly, with rather messy and unpleasant consequences. I eventually realized that one was meant to squat with one's feet on the two plinths which I had taken as a rudimentary low level seat! Inevitably tummy problems

3

followed..... Having been warned not to drink the water, I drank only wine and coffee, mineral water not being on offer in the hostel. Eventually, I was reduced to visiting a nearby Salon du The for an omelette and tea to escape the roughly washed lettuce and rebarbative sausages frequently served in the hostel. I kept company there with Linda, a typist from Rochester, who subsequently became my first girl friend! Back in London, when I visited her basement flat in Holland Park for a drink after I'd taken her out to dinner, I discovered that she had an unfortunate passion for gherkins! This made my attempts to kiss her rather off-putting, although our affair dragged on until she obviously got fed up with my intermittent efforts at communication from Oxford and started writing sarcastic letters, signed "Your obedient servant", and suchlike. A timely warning as to what married life with her would have been like! Some years later we met on the towpath during Eights Week in Oxford. She had a rather pathetic young man in tow, whom she was anxious to show off to me. I gave silent thanks for deliverance!

A couple of years later saw my return to Antibes in very different circumstances. I was about to take up my first teaching post and, on the strength of it, had treated myself to a red and white Triumph Vitesse saloon! Together with a friend from school we motored down through France, to Dijon, before taking the historic Route Napoleon through the French Alps and so down to the Cap d'Antibes. No more youth hostelling! I had seen an advertisement in the personal columns of the *Sunday Times* for B & B in the Chateau des Alpes! It was owned by a nice American family who took in paying guests. Peter and I were installed in a room up in the tower with panoramic views over the Cap. After breakfasting on the lovely terrace we would set off touring the fleshpots of the Cote d"Azur!

So foreign travel began and, a year or two later, I was leading a group of 12 teenage girls and three boys on a tour of Italy for Erna Low's agency.

# 2

# Tour Leader in Italy

The Erna Low Teenage party was to visit three Italian cities: Florence, Rome and Naples. Since I had never visited any of them and couldn't speak Italian, I counted myself very lucky to have been entrusted with the arrangements and supervision of the group! How I ever convinced Miss Low to appoint me I cannot imagine, but she was known as a quixotic and independently minded woman, who quickly made up her mind about those she wished, or did not wish, to employ!

Our group travelled down to Italy by rail. I still remember the thrill of waking up, if one can call it that, after a night of fitful slumber in a six person couchette compartment with the train's wheels grinding away beneath one, to the sight of the Swiss and Italian Alps, as we wound our way down to Milan. There we had to change trains for Florence, inside that great bustling station. Our introduction to the grandeur and chaos of Italy! Many of the trains still had the old wooden seats and compartments, each with its own separate door, that one sees in classic Italian films, like *Rocco and His Brothers,* when the impoverished southerners arrive in Milan on the overnight train from Sicily.

Our arrival in Florence went off well. We found ourselves staying in a lovely pension with magnificent views from its roof-top terrace of the cathedral's great cupola by Brunelleschi. It's now a very expensive 'Boutique' hotel! We were conveniently placed to 'do' all the main sights: the imposing Duomo, the Uffizi Galleries, the Accademia with Michelangelo's original statue of David, the Medici Chapels, Santa Croce, the Annuziata and the charming monks' cells, each decorated with a fresco by Fra Angelico, in nearby San

Marco Monastery. I also acquired a pair of gilded baroque putti and a matching mirror from one of the street markets! I still have them in my retirement flat here in Oxford! After three tremendous days we rejoined the train and moved on down to Rome.

Rome was a bit more difficult, since our hotel was in the distinctly sleazy area alongside Termini Station and 'my' girls were attracting Italian males, who I feared did not always have the best intentions! However, we all survived and managed to tour the Vatican galleries and the Sistine Chapel, as well as St Peter's itself, in those blissful days before mass tourism with its queues, security issues and pressing crowds of uncomprehending orientals glued to their phones and incessantly taking pictures!

My most poignant memories are of a grand café's orchestra playing a throbbing rendition of *Arriverderci Roma* in the huge semicircular Piazza Repubblica, not far from our hotel and Termini Station, and of my first evening visit to the then relatively quiet Trevi Fountain, where the coin I threw in to guarantee my return to Rome has certainly worked! I must have made around a hundred visits at least to the Eternal City over the last 55 years or so, counting visits on ship's tours, as well as longer stays in hotels or at the Venerable English College, where two of my former students have been seminarians.

As we journeyed South to Naples the girls' dresses (in those far-off pre-jeans times!) seemed to get shorter. I think they shortened them each night!

Matters came to a head in Naples, where we found we were to be accommodated in a rather run-down youth hostel in Baia, some way outside Naples, near the Phlegraean Fields of antiquity. There was an old shipyard adjacent to the hostel, and the alleged Roman remains were nowhere to be seen. At night the large double gates to the hostel grounds were firmly locked, but the local youths still thrust their hands through them as they attempted to serenade the 'Ragazze Inglese!'

After a night fighting off the rats on the terrace outside the basement room  that I shared with the three  boys, I called the group together and we took the local Ferrovia Cumana train into Naples and the British Consulate, where we were looked after and taken to the charmingly old-fashioned Pension Pinto Storey, to be given a meal, by arrangement with the Consulate. I telephoned Erna Low (the tour organizer), to say conditions were impossible in the hostel in Baia. I threatened to bring the group back home - perfectly possible since we were travelling by rail with open returns. This really alarmed Miss Low. "Think of the parents' reaction!" she cried, as she hastily arranged coach hire with her local agent Mimi Aloschi (whose family-run company still provides ship's tours from Livorno, Civitavecchia and Naples) to transport our group to Positano for the remaining week.  No doubt my telephoning from the Consulate had impressed upon her the need to do something radical!

In Positano we had makeshift accommodation with camp beds in the half-finished rooms on the top storey of the Villa Nettuno, and meals were provided in a nearby pension. But what a difference from Baia!

Positano, in those far-off days, was extremely chic and not infested with today's hordes of trippers, many of whom now come from cruise ships, of course! The Villa Nettuno was, and is, high up above the Marina Grande Beach. Each day we would wend our way down to the beach and the famous Buca di Bacco café-bar. The beach concession was run from a large red canopy more or less in the centre of the beach by the Lucibello family, who still operate, I believe. They also owned some nice hotels along the coast, like the Marina Riviera in Amalfi.

*View from Villa Nettuno, Positano*

We visited Amalfi from Positano by the old-fashioned coastal steamer that used to ply between Naples and Salerno. The steamer would arrive and drop anchor out in the bay. One would have to reach the ship via a small tender putting out from the shore. Nowadays, a hydrofoil docks at the quayside, provided the sea is not too rough. When it is, the weary day-trippers hoping for a trouble-free return, are faced with a long steep climb up through the village to the coastal road high above. This famous road, the 'Amalfi Drive,' twists and turns its way around the glorious coastline's hairpin bends with dizzying views and sheer drops below. In the summer months the buses are jam-packed and one is lucky to be able to board at all! Often one must wait while 3 or 4 buses pass by, packed to the gills. I well remember an old local lady in her widow's black who reverently made the sign of the cross at each tortuous bend!

Some years later, after a summer job teaching English as a Foreign Language at Westminster College in Oxford, I treated myself to a stay in La Bussola, a favourite hotel of mine in Amalfi, just opposite the harbour. I was delighted to discover that the proprietor's two charming sons had been at that same summer school. That was worth a few Campari sodas in the new hotel bar!

Many years later I was to make the journey by bus from Positano once again, the sea being too rough to permit the hydrofoil to dock. It was some months after the Captain of the *Costa Concordia* had been put under house arrest after his ship had gone aground off the island of Giglio. He had claimed that he 'fell into a lifeboat,' thus conveniently abandoning his ship! It had lately been announced that the former Captain's home was in Sorrento, just along the coast. On board the *Concordia*, he had been showing off to his girl friend, by sailing the vessel dangerously close to the shore in order to 'salute' local friends. Watching the conduct of the bus driver on the Amalfi Drive, who bore a strong resemblance to the disgraced Captain, I speculated as to whether this was his new job! He was flirting with 2 young ladies who were standing on his right, up close to the windscreen, with the bus door wide open behind them. All the while he was smoking cigarettes and also using his mobile phone! Surely this must be the same man! One just hoped he didn't "fall out" of the open front door, should a crash appear imminent!

Whether or not we visited Pompeii on that first unscheduled stay in Positano, three visits since have been more than enough! On the first occasion, our guide asked where my companion and I were from. "Oxford," was the reply. Then he insisted on taking us to view some fading pornographic paintings, normally off tourist limits! He clearly had an unromantic view of the classical interests of Oxford students!

I'm sure we were *meant* to visit Pompeii from Positano, but I think it quite likely that we decided we preferred beach life, or browsing the trendy boutiques that, even then, were blossoming, along the narrow paths that led down to the beach. And Franco Zeffirelli, the great Italian film and opera director, was in his villa just out of Positano in those days. However, we remained unaware of our illustrious neighbour, who had just directed what for my money is the best-ever film of Shakespeare's *Taming of the Shrew* with one of my Oxford contemporaries, the actor Michael York, in the role of Lucentio, to be followed by his Tybalt in *Romeo and Juliet.*

That long ago holiday really opened my eyes to the delights of the Costiera Amalfitana and of Italy, my favourite country. I went on to lead many tours for various agencies to its beautiful cities, and to lecture on most of its many ports.

On my return to England, there was a stiff interview with the formidable Miss Low, together with the Leader of the previous group that had used the same accommodation. "How was it," Miss Low demanded, "that you found conditions at the hostel in Baia so impossible, when the Leader of the previous group had been delighted?" "Well," I suggested, "apart from the rats, the persistent Italian youths outside the gates were a worry to me, being in charge of 12 precocious teenage girls as well as 3 boys." "Nonsense," interjected the somewhat raddled woman who had been the previous Leader. "The local boys were charming, taking the girls out in their boats in the evenings. Everyone, including me, had a wonderful time!" The mind boggled and Miss Low hastily drew our meeting to a close. I heard no more from her after that, but thought it wise to seek other agencies for whom to work, when I had gained more experience of the ins and outs of party leadership!

11

# 3

# First stay in Venice

The firm of Harold Ingham, Ltd (not to be confused with the present firm of Inghams Ltd) was based in Harrow, close to my home in Pinner. Armed with my travel experience with Erna Low, I was able to get myself appointed to revisit Florence and Rome under their auspices as a Tour Leader, or Escort, and also make the first of my many visits to Venice on another tour.

We arrived in Venice by night charter, in the years before such flights were prohibited. To arrive in the middle of the night at the Piazzale Roma, that scruffy staging post at the top of the Grand Canal, where the airport bus deposits you, and then to transfer to water transport was magical. I was rather surprised to find it was a large empty barge that was waiting to waft us and our luggage down the silent canal, flanked by the great palazzi. A few of them were showing just a light here and there, mostly in the upper regions where caretakers or staff lived. It was an unforgettable experience. I can't describe it accurately, since we were tired and travel weary, but it turned out that the barge was usually used to transport vegetables to the Rialto markets, judging from the various items and bits of greenery that were left inside it. And we mostly stood and just gawped as we chugged down the canal to the Salute landing stage.

We were accommodated in a small pension in the Dorsoduro district, or sestier, which takes its name from the firmer ground on which it was built. The pension was the Casa Messner: it still exists, much spruced up. My abiding memory is of being bitten to hell by mosquitoes, which entered my ground floor room through the inadequately

*Venice: the Grand Canal and Madonna della Salute Church*

screened window, which opened on to the calle at the side of the building. The two attractions of our location were that we were close to the Salute church and that, on the way there, was a hospitable and cheap local bar. The church itself is a magnificent Baroque structure by Baldassare Longhena, erected in thanksgiving to Our Lady for deliverance from a terrible plague which ravaged Venice in 1630. And, in spite of the 'hard ground' the district was named after, it required a foundation of no fewer than 1,156,627 wooden piles driven into the mud!

The great Palladian church of Il Redentore, across on the Giudecca island opposite, is a more restrained and elegant building. Its proportions were meticulously planned by Palladio, according to a set of mathematical rules. A sort of Feng Shui of his day! For Palladio and his contemporaries numbers had a mystical appeal, which is now difficult to appreciate. They believed that music and mathematics were closely related and that a study of this relationship would reveal rules to govern proportions in the visual arts.

It had been discovered by the ancients that, if two strings were twanged under identical conditions, the difference in pitch would be one octave, should the shorter be half the length of the longer. It would be a fifth, should it be two thirds the length and a fourth should the relationship be three to four! They therefore concluded that a room in which the shorter wall was one half, two thirds or three quarters of the longer would show a similar harmony through its proportions. It has been said that the buildings of Palladio are therefore as complex and harmonious as a Bach fugue! Feng Shui has nothing on it!

Il Redentore was begun in 1577 and, like the Salute, commemorates deliverance from a plague; in this case, an earlier one. Every year, on the third Sunday in July, the Feast of the Redentore and the anniversary of its foundation, the Doge and Signoria solemnly processed to the church over a bridge of boats from the Zattere. It's one of the few traditions from the Republic that is still kept up. The great bridge of boats is constructed, thereby blocking all access via the Giudecca canal to the port of Venice. During the day the Venetians visit the church, and then there are great firework displays in the evening. Everyone who has a boat is on the water all night, feasting on Mori del Redentore – the traditional mulberries. Then they often row or steam over to the Lido to greet the dawn. One is tempted to wonder what kind of memorial our present age might choose when we are, please God, finally delivered from Covid-19!

Our guide for the duration of our stay was an elderly Venetian gentleman by the name of Dottore Ortolani, who proved to be expert in his field. He conducted us around all

14

the main artistic sights of his city. But first we started off with lecture in the newish Fondazione Cini, established in the former monastic buildings of Palladio's other great church of San Giorgio, situated on its own little island opposite San Marco.

The foundation was established by Count Vittorio Cini in memory of his son, Giorgio, who was tragically killed in a plane accident near Cannes in 1949. Count Cini had been prominent in Mussolini's Fascist party, holding various positions until 1943, when he resigned to plot against Mussolini's dictatorship. When the Nazis occupied Northern Italy he was duly arrested and sent to Dachau. His son Giorgio managed to get him out by bribing officials with gold and jewellery. Our lectures at the Foundation prepared us for an intensive and illuminating week of visits.

My own favourite visit was to the relatively little-known Scuola (Confraternity) of San Giorgio degli Schiavoni, hidden away behind the great Renaissance church of San Zaccaria. It was the home of a confraternity of slavs, or

*Scuola di San Giorgio degli Schiavoni, Venice: S. Jerome &*

Dalmations, mostly merchants trading with the Levant. Their simple little building contains one of the greatest treasures of Venice: a frieze of paintings by Vittorio Carpaccio. It's the only one of his five cycles of paintings to survive in the place, in this case the Scuola, for which it was executed. The pictures (all but two) show stories of the three protectors of Dalmatia: S. George, S. Tryphon and S. Jerome. They show a masterful use of colour and bring out the surfaces of the rare marbles, opulent silks and velvets. Quintessentially Venetian! And Carpaccio also displays a charming sense of humour; for instance, in the scene where St Jerome's very tame lion flusters a group of Dominicans in a delicate pattern of their black and white habits. There's a sense of child-like wonder in his paintings, but they are also very carefully composed. Even today, we still see Venice partly through his eyes, in all its colour and luxury.

The two greatest paintings of the sixteenth century in Venice, or anywhere in the world, are, in my opinion, Titian's *Assumption of the Virgin* over the high altar of the majestic Frari church and Tintoretto's almost overpoweringly powerful *Crucifixion* in the nearby Scuola San Rocco. Both impressed themselves on my mind so deeply on that first visit that I have returned to them again and again, on subsequent visits to Venice.

As for buildings, the vast thirteenth century Dominican church of SS Giovanni e Paolo (or Zanipolo in Venetian dialect) holds pride of place for sheer grandeur, and its array of Doge's tombs. But the little jewel-box of the fifteenth century Santa Maria dei Miracoli - surely one of the most beautiful buildings in the world - and the baroque opulence of the Gesuiti , with its damask-patterned marble interior, up in the North of the city, near the Fondamenta Nuova, are my favourites.

# 4

# First Steps in Public Speaking

I had already discovered the attractions of public speaking while in the Sixth Form at my London school, when I started to attend the meetings of the Freston Society - the school's Debating club. Although I was a shy youth, it began to dawn on me that I could gain the attention of an audience of my peers, and even hold it, by going out on a limb and taking up extreme positions on the topics we debated. And I confess I enjoyed such attention.

So, when I went up to St John's College, I started speaking at the College Debating Society. I particularly remember one passionately argued motion that 'This House would hang Sir Oswald Mosley.' It was proposed by one of my fellow historians, a Jewish boy from Highgate School in North London, and opposed by me. The proposer's father was a famous lawyer with extreme left-wing leanings. He had defended the Communists who were attempting to take over the Electrical Trades Union in those distant days of union power. His son, like another Highgate boy in our year, was also a dedicated Marxist. As a rather priggish Young Conservative and member of the University's Conservative Association, I was naturally opposed to anything he supported.

But I had another motive in opposing the motion, in that Sir Oswald's son Max was up at Christ Church at that time and his father had visited the University and even spoken, amid rowdy scenes, at the Oxford Union. I was attracted to his charismatic speaking and his idea of a United Europe, as a third force against both American and Russian power. Max was Secretary of the OU Strasbourg Club, a pro-Europe club with some interesting members. One such was Michel, a French lad whose father had fought in the OAS (the movement to keep Algeria French) in Algeria. A few years later I was able to visit Michel and his interesting family in their lovely house at Cavalaire on the French Riviera. As 'pieds noirs' (people of French or other European origin who had been born in Algeria when it was under French rule) they had been forced to leave their home and livelihood in Algeria when General de Gaulle granted the country its independence in 1962. Since the General had been returned to power from his self-imposed exile at Colombey-les-Deux-Eglises with the backing of the diehard Algerie Francais movement they felt betrayed. "I understand you," he had famously assured them in a speech on 4th June 1958.

Through another Committee member, I was invited to meet Max's father, Sir Oswald Mosley, and his beautiful and fascinating mother, Diana, one of the famous Mitford sisters, in their London flat in Lowndes Square. As I remember, when their white-coated butler leant over the dining table to serve us at dinner, a distinct bulge of a revolver in its holster was visible inside his jacket. But perhaps I've imagined this! There were certainly enough people around in those days who would like to have shot Sir Oswald, since he was the former Leader of the British Union of Fascists, now called 'Union Movement.'

The hatred which the mention of Mosley's name could still invoke 20 years after his and Lady Mosley's imprisonment as security risks, during the Second World War, was vividly illustrated when a thoughtless, or possibly mischievous remark by one of my college friends to the effect that I was entertaining Sir Oswald and his son to drinks in my ground floor rooms in St John's drew a militant mob who started shouting and banging on my sported oak (the stout outer door with which older college rooms were equipped to ensure privacy whilst one was studying, or possibly engaged in less uplifting activities). Prominent amongst the mob was another St John's man who was editor of the student newspaper *Cherwell*. He went on to become a distinguished journalist and Editor by turns of *The Economist*, *The Times* and the London *Evening Standard*.

I later put it around that Sir Oswald had escaped the ravening mob through my ground floor window, which opened on to the Front Quad, round the corner from the staircase that gave access to my rooms, but I must confess this was a bit of imaginative embroidery on my part, since the sought-after speaker was nowhere to be seen. This didn't stop *Cherwell* running a lurid headline, 'Mosleyites Move In on Strasbourg Club.' I consulted my distinguished Tutor, the historian Sir Keith Thomas, about this slur and he wisely told me I must insist on a printed apology for this calumny, since it might come back to haunt me in my future career. This I duly obtained from *Cherwell,* just in case I should ever need to produce it, but that has not - so far - proved to be necessary!

Later the Mosleys moved to settle permanently in France in the 'Temple de La Gloire,' quite near the Duke and Duchess of Windsor's residence, with whom they were friendly. I had no further contact with them or the Movement.

From these beginnings, I had been emboldened to join the OU Conservative Association's Speakers' Classes; which, in those distant days when the Church of England could still be described as 'the Tory party at prayer,' were pleasantly accommodated each week in the Orangery of the Dean's Garden in Christ Church. Our teacher was a vicar's wife called Stella Gatehouse, who used to come in from Deddington on the bus each week. After our training session we would take it in turn to walk her back, with her enormous handbag, to the bus station. Edward Heath and Margaret Thatcher were both former pupils.

After some months' progress, the next stage was to join a panel of speakers from OUCA at a local Conservative meeting. 'Local' included venues as far away as Stroud in Gloucestershire, I remember! These evenings followed the same form as the BBC's 'Any Questions.' I noticed my own modest contributions, usually well to the Right of the other undergraduate panel members, several of whom went on to become MPs, seemed to go down best with the local audiences!

I even spoke in a debate at the Oxford Union, which was about Africa and demands in Kenya for Freedom or 'Uhuru'- a word I made much of in my speech. To this day, there is an ethnic grocer's shop in Oxford's Cowley Road with the same name! I have not so far investigated its offerings!

*Oxford Union Society Debate*

As Steward of the University Conservative Association (OUCA), which had hired the premises of the Union for a meeting, I was in charge of security in the debating chamber, while grander Committee members entertained the then Prime Minister, Harold Macmillan, to dinner in the Oxford Union dining room, before he addressed the assembled crowd in the Debating Chamber. There was a large mob in the garden between the building that housed the dining room and the chamber. They were demonstrating in favour of Nuclear Disarmament. The Prime Minister became separated from his policeman (I think there was only one!) and the other diners. Eventually I heard, from outside the door, a quavering voice beseeching us: "Please let me in, I'm the Prime Minister!" Having complied with his request and his having been pulled around the half-opened door, he was so shaken that he referred in his speech to the 'League of Nations,' instead of the 'United Nations!'

On another occasion, when I had climbed the dizzy heights of the OUCA Committee a little further, as Dinner Secretary, we entertained the Russian Ambassador, who – unlike Mr Macmillan - arrived with a posse of grim-looking security men. We had laid in a plentiful supply of Stolichnaya vodka (the real Russian stuff) to entertain the party suitably. But they were obviously under strict instructions to avoid any traps, so they stuck to water throughout the meal. At one point, after consuming a good share of 'their' vodka, I attempted to pour some red wine for them but missed their glasses and sloshed it on the tablecloth. I remember commenting, "Well, at least it's the right colour," but can remember nothing more of that evening!

Dr Fisher, the then Archbishop of Canterbury, and his wife, were our guests on another occasion in the Union Dining Room and I remember the gentle way in which His Grace sent up my attempt at sophistication by putting the menu cards into (doubtless) rather dreadful French. 'Dindoneau' (aka Turkey) caused particular amusement! The Archbishop's wife had been at Sherborne Girls' School with our Speakers' Class's tutor, so they were able to reminisce happily together about their schooldays, down in Dorset.

# 5

# My introduction to P & O and Chandris Cruises

My closest friend at College, Nick, was not politically minded: he was much more interested in fast cars. As undergraduates, we roared around the Oxfordshire countryside in his MG, his TR2, his XK150 and, finally, his E-type Jag, from one country pub restaurant to another. Tops was 'Dirty Dudley's,' a wonderful pub on the Faringdon road at Kingston Bagpuize. Its real name was the 'Lamb and Flag,' which betokened a link with, if not outright ownership by, our college, St John's. Dudley Laer, the landlord, sported an enormous stomach, held in place by an army belt. He employed a rustic maiden as a skivvy. He was, we learnt, an Old Boy of Brighton College, a minor public school down on the Sussex coast whose current Headmaster has achieved fame by permitting those boys who wish to come to school in skirts to do so! Reverting to Dudley (whose girth would certainly not have suited a skirt) his great charisma and bonhomie manifested itself in his charming custom of inviting guests to tot up their own bills. They were never disputed!

As Nick and I screeched round the roundabout one evening, at the top of the Banbury Road in North Oxford, close to where I now live, there was a searing noise and we found ourselves in the car, sliding along the Banbury Road in a shower of sparks. One of the front wheels had sheared off and gone bowling down the road of its own accord! We emerged shaken but whole.

Nick died young, not, as you might expect, in a car accident, but in a parachute jump, while training with the Territorial Army. We had both belonged to the Oxford University Officers' Training Corps, in my case solely for the pleasant club facilities to which this gave access, but Nick had continued to serve in the volunteer Territorial Army when he became a schoolmaster at a preparatory school in Eastbourne, after going down from Oxford. The memorial garden bench for which his friends subscribed still stands, with its inscription, in St John's College gardens.

Nick's girl friend Jane did the classic thing after his death and went off to sea to drown her sorrows as a WAP (Woman Assistant Purser, in those days) with the P & O shipping line. I went down to join her for dinner aboard the old *Arcadia* (there have been 2 more recent ones) in Tilbury docks- P & O's old home port on the Thames, dating back to colonial days. I was introduced over drinks to John Batterbee, who was Entertainment Officer (there were no 'Cruise Directors' then) on board *Arcadia.* He subsequently became Head of P & O's Entertainment Department ashore and I asked him if he could give me a chance as a Port Lecturer on board one of the Company's ships.

At that time, around 1965, P & O Orient Line, as it was then known, was still operating line voyages, mostly to our former colonies. The larger, newer ships *SS Canberra* and *SS Oriana* (flagship of the former Orient Line, controlled by P & O since the 1920s and one of the fastest liners at sea) still did the Australia run, and the smaller vessels- *SS Arcadia, SS Iberia, SS Orsova, SS Oronsay, SS Orcades, SS Himalaya, SS Chusan* and the little *Chitral* were mixing line voyages to India and the Far East with cruises to cover fallow periods. They often sailed half empty- absolute bliss if you were in First Class! 'P & O never mix the Classes,' one was firmly told. Passage for crew members between the First and Tourist sections of the vessel was usually through a back door in the serving area of a bar, which opened on to another bar of the other class on the opposite side. There were also some doors in the companionways (never 'corridors') with forbidding notices to deter would-be trespassers! However, the two oldest ships, *Himalaya* and *Orcades,* had already been opened up as one class ships: a foretaste of the future. I was told later that they were the only ships that made any money!

Even before my introduction to P & O, I had already got myself a couple of free passages with Chandris cruises, forerunner of the present Celebrity brand. A London travel firm called *Bachelors Abroad* used to arrange parties of single people - many more spinsters and widows than bachelors, I'm afraid - to sail on cruises with an escort (me!) to facilitate introductions and generally oil the social wheels. The term 'Escort' didn't carry the connotations then that it has since acquired! In return for his services the escort got a free passage.

So one Easter holiday saw me meeting my party at Gatwick airport, preparatory to our flying to Venice to join the *SS Fiesta,* one of Chandris Cruises' three little cruise ships at that time. What a mixed bag they were! About a dozen women and three men made up the group.

*Fiesta* had actually been built at Cammell Laird's famous yard in Belfast for the Isle of Man Steam Packet Company in1946. She was skillfully converted in 1964 by the Greek owners of the Chandris line for economy Mediterranean cruises. Her gross tonnage was only 3,659- one tenth of the GRT of a small luxury cruise ship of today!

After landing at Venice's Marco Polo airport, we were transferred into that magical city via the long road bridge built parallel to the railway bridge in Mussolini's time. *Fiesta* was moored at the San Basilio quay, at the top of the wide Giudecca Canal, opposite the Molino Stucky, that great forbidding 19th century gothic-style flour mill, now converted into a Hilton hotel and apartments. Forty years later I was to sail often from the same berth in one of the former *Yachts of Seabourn,* before their larger current replacements made it necessary for them to dock in the huge Bacino della Stazione Marittima, around the top of the Fusina canal, where the monster cruise ships still dock. For how much longer I know not. There is a great deal of vocal local opposition to their being allowed so close to this precious city. Fortunately, at the time of writing, Silversea still retains four of their older vessels that can dock at San Basilio, as can the older Seabourn ships. From there one can simply stroll out of the terminal building and cross a little bridge to immerse oneself in one of the most charming and least spoilt districts of Venice. There were, and still are, several little trattorie along the Fondamenta Nani, beside a side canal, that are favoured by ships' crews when they are there overnight.

*Chandris Cruises' **Fiesta** at Venice 1966*

When it is time to sail, usually in the evening, one has the magnificent experience of sailing down the Giudecca Canal, with the three great Palladian churches: Il Redentore, the smaller Zitelle and finally proud San Giorgio on its own little island to starboard, while to port one sails by the Zattere promenade with its restaurants and pizzerias, past the Gesuati church with the Accademia galleries behind it, towards the dome of the Salute church, like a great moored balloon guarding the entrance to port of the Grand Canal and its palaces. Just before that, I usually point out La Calcina pension (where John Ruskin the art critic and author of *The Stones of Venice* stayed). Next, also on the port side, one passes the back of the Salute church, then the old Custom House and the opening to the Grand Canal, before one sees the Piazzetta, opening on to St Mark's Square, with its iconic basilica, once the private chapel of the Doges, with their palace next door. And so it goes, passing the Riva Schiavoni to port with its great hotels and the church of Santa Maria della Pieta, with its adjoining former orphanage, famous for the singing of its girls who performed under the direction of no less a master than Antonio Vivaldi from 1703 to 1745.

Then one passes by an old working class quarter to port, with fine displays of washing, strung across Via Garibaldi. Finally come the Giardini, where the Venice Biennale (the Art exhibition) is held every two years, and, last, St. Elena island, with its ancient monastery, modern naval college and – surprisingly - Venice's football stadium.

On the starboard side, by now the Lido island comes into view with the 1930s-style dome of the Templo Votivo, built between 1925 and 1935, during the Mussolini era, as a memorial to Italy's War Dead of the First World War, next to the little ancient church of S. Maria Elisabetta, with which it is often confused. Then the ship sweeps round to starboard to take the middle exit channel, the Porta del Lido, from the Lagoon into the Adriatic Sea.

Every year here, for about eight centuries from the middle of the twelfth century, there was the elaborate ceremony of Venice's Marriage to the Sea. It began as a way of commemorating the adventures of Doge Pietro Orseolo II, who had set sail on Ascension Day 1000 to subjugate the pestilential pirates of the Dalmatian coast. His standard was the Lion of St Mark with its paw on an open book, which was to become the emblem of Venice. The Doge and his Court sailed down in the Bucintoro, the elaborate state barge depicted in so many Venetian paintings, with an escort of decorated vessels. Then a golden ring was dropped into the ocean and everyone disembarked for a Solemn Mass in the church of San Nicolo al Lido.

Nowadays, as one's ship negotiates the channel to the open sea, one has a close view of the works, known as 'MOSE' – Modulo Sperimentale Elettromeccanico - and also a reference to the biblical figure Moses, who parted the Red Sea to enable the Israelites to flee to safety from Egypt. The idea is to keep high tides out and avoid the persistent flooding of Venice during the times of the Aqua Alta. It was first designed back in 1984, but progress has been painfully slow, due to corruption. Work didn't begin until 2003. The project was due to be finished by 2016, but that date has now been put back until 2021. The total cost, including all expenses, is estimated at €7 billion. Meanwhile, every November and Spring, the waters return to reclaim for a time large areas of the city, including St Mark's Square itself. One has to negotiate one's progress on duckboards in waterproof boots!

# 6

# Croatian and Greek memories

Aboard *Fiesta* our group was closely packed into the compact accommodation on board. My task was to keep the members happy, if possibly by effecting introductions between them, while looking out for any spare men to dance and socialize with my ladies in the evenings!

I'm afraid the three male members of the group were not very promising material for their putative role as Lotharios, consisting as they did of a 60-something gentleman, described on the list I was given of participants, as a 'Company Director,' but who turned out to be merely the proprietor of a launderette! Then there was a middle-aged schoolmaster, who taught in a prep school quite close to my school in Kent. Patrick, with his droll sense of humour, dapper turn-out, always with a silk handkerchief on show in his top jacket pocket, and mellifluous tones was to become one of my lifetime friends. He sadly died during his annual winter stay last year in the Philippines, after falling in his bathroom. I still badly miss our lunches together in his London club and his wise words of advice, freely offered to a younger colleague.

As for the third, rather nondescript man in our group, I have to confess I can remember nothing about him at all!

My main role as Escort was to oil the wheels at the dinner table by helping conversation along. I'm still doing this on board Seabourn cruise ships as a 'Guest Conversationalist' (as Lecturers have been rebranded) nearly 60 years on! One is not allowed to discuss religion or politics, according to one's "Agreement" (a contract with no payment). Just as well, in the times of President Trump! Fortunately I am spared finding dancing partners for the ladies! Or, even worse, having to dance with them, like the professional 'Dance Hosts'- or gigolos, as I unfairly call them - aboard the Cunard, Crystal and Fred Olsen ships. These poor guys have the most dangerous job aboard, since they must keep the often formidably determined, even predatory, ladies happy, while carefully avoiding any hint of favouritism between them. And there is strictly no hanky-panky allowed! To ensure this, the escorts are accommodated in pairs down in their cabins! But the days of the 'Gay Gordons' and the 'Dashing White Sergeant' dances with my mother in the old ships' ballrooms are long gone, even in the grand ballrooms still to be found aboard the Cunard liners!

Returning to *Fiesta,* from Venice we sailed down the Adriatic towards Greece and her islands, cruising past what was still Yugoslavia in those distant days. Its ruler, Marshall Tito, was a Communist who had come to power by leading resistance to the German invaders during the Second World War. For some perverse reason, the late satirical novelist Evelyn Waugh, who had served there on the British side, along with Winston Churchill's errant son Randolph, always maintained that Tito was, in fact, a woman!

This wildly implausible theory contrasted greatly with the dour regime over which the Marshal presided. All the larger hotels and restaurants were state-run enterprises, which resulted in a depressing uniformity. Staying with a friend in the pleasant little resort of Cavtat, just down the coast from Dubrovnik, a few years later, we sought a change from the monotonous hotel cuisine by going out to a local restaurant. To our disappointment we discovered that they all appeared to offer exactly the same depressing menu! Not only that- the waitresses were all dressed exactly the same as those in our hotel, even down to the unglamorous but serviceable little boots they all wore! They had an interesting concept of restaurant service too. When we requested a table for two we were led to a table for four, where two places had already been used, as evinced by the plates with remains of the unappetizing food left on the table. It proved impossible to get these cleared before we had finished our own meals. Tables were only to be cleared once! The food was trundled up to the tables on trolleys, pushed by the grim waitresses.

We found the same system in force when we moved down the coast to our second Yugoslav hotel, on the delightful island of Korcula. But here we encountered another problem. We had, as usual, booked ourselves two separate rooms. On arrival at the hotel Reception desk, we were greeted with the news that only one double room was available. This was a problem one met frequently in more unsophisticated resorts in the 1960s, and we had developed ways of dealing with it. One precaution was to register separately as 'Mr' and 'Miss," although my friend declined to travel in drag, so it was not always a successful plan, should one meet an intransigent desk clerk. Our next ploy was to refuse to contemplate even one night in the shared room offered. (They always hoped that, after the first night, one would settle down and accept it.)

"I'm afraid it's quite impossible for us to share, for health reasons," I would announce, while looking at my friend in a meaningful manner, as if to say, "He's highly infectious!" "We very sorry- only have one double room," was the unyielding response from the clerk of the Hotel Marko Polo in Korcula. "Well, I'm afraid we've had a long tiring day travelling down here and we need to get some sleep now," I retorted. So we both began to undress, there and then, in front of the reception desk, while eyeing the sofas in the lounge in a meaningful manner. At that point the hotel clerk sprang into action, "Ah...one moment gentlemen, let me just check

…. Oh yes, I think another room has become available if you would like to follow me…" (the one they were keeping back in the hope of a desperate last-minute customer whom they could fleece). This scene was to be played out more than once more in various hotel lobbies in years to come!

On another occasion, on the Greek island of Spetse, we were faced with the usual problem, in spite of a clear reservation for two separate rooms. This time we were able to telephone our travel agent in London, who tore a strip off the wheedling proprietor of the rather grubby pension we were booked into, for not fulfilling his contract. So effective was this that we found ourselves transferred to the first class Hotel Posidonian Palace! This proved, back in those early days, to be a charmingly traditional hotel constructed in the late nineteenth century in a vague imitation of a French chateau. There was, of course, no suggestion of air conditioning, although it was the height of the Greek summer heat. But there was a very adequate, if somewhat alarming substitute. During the afternoon siesta, the custom was to leave the door of one's room propped open to get a through air current, with a chintz-covered screen erected in the doorway to protect the modesty of the at most lightly glad occupants, prone on their beds. It was good sport, after a few drinks with lunch, to return upstairs and attempt to push each other through the screens into the rooms of the startled resting ladies!

Dinner was an amusing occasion. Each evening the Directeur (as the manager was pretentiously titled) would supervise the transfer of all the dining tables from the hotel's restaurant out onto the terrace! At the end of the evening all the tables and chairs were carried back inside by the heavily breathing waiters. The menus were, naturally, all in French - just like my menus for the University Conservative Association back in college days! My memories of the food are that each course seemed to be goat-flavoured! The pungent Greek Feta cheese was one thing, but when it followed goat stew and the butter was also goat, to say nothing of the milk, it all got a bit much! Cow's milk was virtually unobtainable in Greece in the 1960s- even in the Posidonian Palace Hotel! And the crowning incident was when we hired a boatman to take us on a trip round the island. When we had been going for a little while I became aware of a distinct whiff of that all-pervasive goat smell! Was I now imagining it everywhere? No! Down below, in the boat's little cabin, was the sweetest little goat - the Captain's pet! But even that didn't convert me to the goat cuisine!

Returning to my first cruise, I suppose the highpoint must remain my first ascent of the Acropolis in Athens. *Fiesta* was berthed in the port of Piraeus, then, as now, a busy, bustling place, with all the island ferries disgorging their passengers, locals and tourists, mostly young, from the huge doors at the rear of the ferries. Many of them would be making for the taxi queues and the inevitable negotiations that would follow. Touts would scan the queues offering rides in unlicensed and often decrepit vehicles at "special" prices. The youngsters would often be travelling with huge back-packs, boots dangling from the sides and perhaps a teapot hanging from a strap. I well remember attempting to join a ferry in Mykonos, in the days when one had to travel out to the ship in a local boat, before a quay capable of taking ferries and cruise ships was built on the edge of town. As I attempted to climb the ladder up the ship's side from our boat I was repeatedly knocked around the head by the teapot dangling from the bag of the young lady up ahead of me!

The easiest way to get into central Athens from Piraeus, if one is not impeded with heavy baggage, is by the little railway that runs direct from the port. These days it has been incorporated into an impressive new Metro system, part of the city's preparations for the Olympics back in 2004 at a cost of nearly 9.000 million Euros, including a brand new airport. If one alights at Monastiraki station it is fairly easy to make one's way up through the old Plaka district,

*Athens: The Parthenon*

with its restaurants, pensions and tourist shops, to the Acropolis itself. Back in the early 1960s it was not necessary to pay for admission- you just climbed up though the Propylaea, taking care on the large, irregular steps polished smooth by the millions of tourists who have followed the same route over the centuries. And, once you were through the entrance, there before you was the most famous building in the world- the ancient Parthenon of Athens. It's artfully sited, above and at an angle, so one corner of the building faces you and you can see the whole extent of that great temple to Athena,, the goddess and protector of Athens, as you enter. It's one of Life's great experiences. When I came with my mother some years later she insisted, to my consternation, on making the climb, popping her Angina pills under her tongue as she went!

Another great, but very different, experience on that first cruise was our call at Chios, one of the North Eastern Aegean islands, close to the Turkish coast. It proved to be a delightfully unspoilt and fertile island. But why had Chandris decided upon *this* island, out of so many? The answer soon became obvious - it was the home island of the Chandris Line's founder, Anthony Chandris, who, with his brother Dimitris, controlled what was by then the largest fleet in the world! Younger members of the family soon appeared on board and were proudly given a conducted tour of what was then a relatively 'new' vessel, or at least a newly converted one! Since those days the Chandris family has even opened their own hotel - the Chandris, the first luxury hotel on the island. I believe the family still owns it. Sadly Chios is now also the location of one of Greece's largest migrant camps.

The second Chandris cruise ship I sailed in was the slightly larger ex-Irish ferry renamed *Fantasia,* which turned out to be of even more venerable lineage than *Fiesta*, having been launched as the *Duke of York* by the old LMS railway back in 1935! She had taken part in the Normandy landings during the Second World War and was just 1,000 odd tons larger than *Fiesta*. I can still recall a terrifying Adriatic storm that we endured, when all doors to the deck outside had to be locked, and the ship pitched and tossed so much that I feared she would capsize, if we weren't struck by the lightning that lit up the sky above. Since that experience I have held the Adriatic and the storms to which it is prone in considerable respect!

Checking the history of former Chandris ships on line while writing this, I was struck by the number of their ships that came to grief one way or the other, including *Fantasia,* which caught fire in 1976, thus bringing her second career to an abrupt end 41 years after she had been first launched.

# 7

# P & O: the Empire's Line

While still working with Bachelors Abroad, I was able to move a little upmarket ship-wise, escorting one of their parties aboard P & O's *Oronsay* in 1968. She was a lovely old ship, around 27,000 GRT, built for the Orient Line (all their ships' names began with 'Or') in 1950. She was their second new ship after WW2, sister to the earlier (1947) *Orcades.*

*P & O's **Oronsay** at Gibraltar c.1968*

Our group was accommodated in Tourist Class, at the after end of the ship, but one evening I was able to sneak through the barrier to explore the forbidden territory of the First Class deck area. I was greatly impressed by the spacious areas, with practically no-one in sight. No doubt they were all dressing for dinner: black tie was still very much *de rigueur* in First Class in the Sixties and Seventies! There were rigid, but unwritten, rules about this: *never* dress on the first night! Steamer trunks had perhaps not yet arrived in one's cabin, or been unpacked. Never in port - and in those far-off days we were often moored for an evening or overnight stay. And, finally, never on the last night, since one would have packed one's bags, ready for disembarkation the following morning! It was a bit of a minefield for the uninitiated, although one could obtain a little book of shipboard etiquette, should one be prepared to admit one's uncertainty about such esoteric matters! There were always a few unfortunates who had got it wrong! Another little refinement was that white dinner jackets, or tuxedos as our American friends call them, could be worn, once we entered the Med, but NOT on the way down or the journey back, up the coast of North-west Spain and Portugal and through the often choppy Bay of Biscay. The ship's officers used to follow a similar custom, by changing into whites once we reached the Med.

Disembarkation at the end of the cruise was a much more leisurely affair back in those days. We didn't usually dock in Southampton until 8 or 9am. If we had met bad weather in the English Channel it could be even later. Then all the bags would have to be laboriously unloaded. Ships still had vast holds below decks and steamer trunks and bulkier items could be stowed down there by the crew. Regular sized bags were kept up on deck overnight in piles on the after-deck for the last night of the cruise. Once the ship had been made fast in the morning they would be unloaded by crane in vast netted bundles. Then they had to be sorted ashore by the heavily unionised dockers, if they weren't on strike! They frequently were! If that was the case the Company's office staff would be pressed into service. On one occasion the ship had actually to be diverted to Portsmouth to be able to dock and unload. If a strike prevented ships being properly provisioned at Southampton the necessary supplies would be driven down to North West Spain and loaded instead at Vigo or Corunna! No wonder the unions nearly brought the port of Southampton to its knees!

This leisurely disembarkation meant there was always time for a "full English" breakfast on the last morning in the Dining Room! It was often around 10 or 11am before the luggage was all ashore and sorted and disembarkation could commence. After one had located one's bags, if one was lucky one could find a porter to wheel them through Customs for a tip, avoiding the piercing eyes of the Customs officers as one followed, and hoping the extra duty-free bottles one had concealed amongst one's laundry would remain safe and undetected.

The ships in those days always had an overnight stay for turn-around in Southampton, which was good for crew with local families. Staff would come down from the P & O offices in London to stay overnight on board in order to do the next morning's embarkation. This made for much more civilized conditions all round. I often think that the hurried cleaning of the ship that now has to take place between the departure of guests no later than 9am (so much for the fond farewells!) and the arrival of the new set from about noon onwards may be contributory to the frequency of outbreaks of norovirus on board! However, I have been assured by the ship's Doctor that it is usually the result of older passengers' failure to wash their hands after visiting the lavatory!

When the time came for the ship to sail most of the passengers would come up on deck to witness the spectacle. There would be a band - often the Royal Marines - to play us off. A mixture of popular and martial - or naval - music was played. I always found, 'A Life on the Ocean Wave,' 'Rule Britannia' and 'We are Sailing" particularly moving, as the great ship got under way and the gap between us and the quayside increased, bridged, in those far-off days by thick strands of paper streamers, until the band saluted smartly, about-turned and marched off, as we slipped down Southampton Water towards Spithead and the English Channel.

Another benefit of the overnight stay in port was that there would always be at least one decent spare cabin available that had been used by the embarkation staff. This was a godsend when I was accompanied on board in later years by my widowed mother. As soon as it was realized that she was NOT my wife (and she was very loathe to be thought of as a 'cradle-snatcher' as she put it!) a spare cabin would be found for her. That held good until our very last voyage together in *Canberra*!

Our cruise in *Oronsay* took us down to the Med from Southampton, stopping off first in Lisbon, a city whose allure never alters. Back in the 1960s Portugal was still under the iron hand of Dr Antonio Salazar, the Economics don from Coimbra University who had come to power back in 1932. He had suffered a cerebral haemorrhage in 1968 and had been replaced as Prime Minister by Dr Caetano. But he died without knowing he had been replaced as Premier. Fearing the shock might kill him, his doctors and colleagues did not tell him that Marcello Caetano had been installed as Premier. They kept up a charade of talking with Salazar as though he were still head of state, nodding accord to his directives. He was denied access to newspapers, radio and television on the ground that they might overtire him.

Occasionally, Salazar would appear in public in a wheel chair. He continued to live in the Premier's official residence, from which his successor refused to dislodge him, and eventually he died peacefully in his chair on the beach at Estoril, just down the River Tagus estuary from Lisbon, in 1970.

Salazar was responsible for the Estado Novo, the corporatist authoritarian government that continued to rule Portugal until 1974. In that year the so-called 'Carnation Revolution' swept his successor, Dr Caetano, from power, in a mass rising supported by left-wing Army officers. The carnations were stuck into the barrels of the rifles carried by the troops, to proclaim their wish for a peaceful Revolution. Lisbon changed almost overnight from being a beautifully kept city, with its grand and pristine buildings, into a heavily graffiti-daubed and scruffy place. A ring of shanty towns grew up suddenly on the city's outskirts, housing the many who, armed with their Portuguese nationality, came to settle from the newly independent former Portuguese colonies of Angola, Mozambique, Goa and Macau.

*Ponte 25 Abril, Lisbon*

The great Salazar Bridge, opened in 1966, which spanned the Tagus and opened up the formerly impoverished South to tourism (a mixed blessing to anyone who remembers the Algarve before all the high-rise development) was renamed the Bridge of the 25th April, the date of the Revolution. It has taken many years for the city to recover and digest all the new arrivals. Now it spreads all along the Tagus, as one sails towards the ship's berth, formerly at Alcantara, in the shadow of the great bridge, with its perpetual buzzing sound from the tyres of the vehicles passing overhead. A new cruise terminal has been constructed in the last few years further upstream, on the site of some old South American tobacco warehouses - Jardim de Tobacco. It's another reminder of Portugal's great imperial and maritime past.

Having 'upgraded' from escorting in Chandris ships to P & O ships, my next aim was to get an appointment on board a P & O liner as Port Lecturer. I had made a point of attending some of the Port Lectures aboard *Oronsay* in order to get an idea of what was required. They were given by a rather formidable old girl called Mrs J Howard Cusworth. It was said she had been a P & O nanny in the Twenties and, more recently, she was the Cambridge opposite number of Stella Gatehouse, my Oxford University Conservative Association Speakers' Class tutor. So we got on rather well. I was very impressed by her cabin in First Class aboard *Oronsay*, complete with sea water bath, and a little basin of fresh water above it for washing one's face! "Drinking' water (if one dared) was supplied to cabins in Thermos jugs. I shunned them, except for teeth cleaning!.In those days Gin was almost cheaper on board than the Tonic water with which one topped it up!

Mrs Howard Cusworth's lectures were not State of the Art. Faded slides (which I later discovered could be supplied by P & O if one was short of pictures) were pushed through an ancient projector by a young lady from the Bureau (the ship's Reception desk and office - where the WAPS were!) on the imperious call, "Next one, dear!" The attendances usually dwindled as the cruise progressed, often ending as a small gathering of other ladies around the projector, who wanted to know where one could get 'a nice cup of tea' ashore! And each talk had to be given at least twice - once in each class! And, as I discovered later, it had to be given three times in *Canberra,* before the days of video recording! (Twice for the much greater number of Tourist class passengers, who were admitted to the cinema through different doors to First Class passengers!) In the *QE2,* in the old days, First Class ('Grill') passengers sat in the cinema balcony, with its separate entrance, safely above the *hoi polloi*!

In the older ships without a cinema, like *Chusan,* the lecture would be given in the First and Tourist ballrooms. Down in the Tourist section, at the after end of the ship, the vibrations from the ship's screws below were often so bad that the projector lens frequently went out of focus and had to be intermittently refocused by the unfortunate assistant. Although only about one third of the passenger accommodation was designated First Class, about two thirds of the deck space was assigned to those fortunate ones. And it was always up front (Forward) and mid-ships, where the First Class pool would be located. The Tourist Class pool would be at the after end of the vessel, well positioned to catch those thick black smuts periodically released from the funnel that had escaped the crowded Tourist sun deck! Deckchairs with arms were provided in First Class, but without in Tourist. A number of seasoned passengers used to bring their own seats on board, as well as their own pillows. I heard that aboard the luxurious all First Class Cunarder *Caronia,* nicknamed the Green Goddess after her eau-de-nil hull, wealthy Americans used to bring all their own furniture for a 3 month voyage.

# 8

# First Love as a Novice Port Lecturer!

*Painting **Chusan's** Funnel*

My first chance as a Port Lecturer came in August 1969. I have already recounted how I had been introduced to John Batterbee on board *Arcadia* in Tilbury Docks a few years previously, when I went down to see my old college friend

Nick's girl friend, who was working on board as a WAP (Woman Assistant Purser) after Nick's tragic death.

After I had gained my shipboard experience in P & O's *Oronsay* and *Orcades* as a Bachelors Abroad Escort, I was emboldened to propose myself to Mr Batterbee as a potential Port Lecturer. In June I was thrilled to get a phone call from him, "There's a vacancy for a Port Lecturer next month aboard *Chusan*. The chap I had already booked has had to withdraw." Naturally, I leapt at the chance and threw myself into preparing my first set of lectures. Since I was also about to move from my first teaching post down in Kent to the heights of Harrow on the Hill and its famous school, I had my work cut out. Fortunately the ports were ones I had already visited on my previous cruises as a Bachelors Abroad Escort and I was also able to eke out my meagre collection of slides with a selection kindly supplied by P & O. A few years later P & O appointed a chap who had worked for Kodak, and was therefore something of a photographic expert, to take over their ageing slide collection and expand it with some good new slides. But that was still a way off. Later on I developed a useful working partnership with another Port Lecturer, so we could borrow each other's slides for ports we were short on. But he told me years later he never lent me his best pictures and (guess what!) I had to confess the same!

I had already got my first glimpse of, and fallen in love with, *Chusan* when she was moored alongside the Riva Schiavoni, just past the Doge's Palace and the grand hotels in Venice. Design work on her had begun back in 1946, soon after the end of the war, as a replacement for P & O's famous *Viceroy of India,* which had been lost in the war. *Chusan* was the largest (at just over 26,000GRT) and last ship built for P & O's Far East services, a destination already looking questionable by the time of her launching, and even more so by the time I joined her.

When she entered service in 1950 she was the first passenger ship to be equipped with anti-roll stabilisers. But air conditioning wasn't installed until a refit in 1960! Since she had already undertaken P & O's first ever World Cruise in 1954, I imagine the tickets marked 'POSH' (standing for 'Port Out and Starboard Home, being the shaded sides of the ship in each direction) were at a premium! Not only did P & O give the word 'posh' to the English language, but they also used it as the name of their incentive club for past travellers – the 'Posh Club!' If you Google that now you find it is shown as referring to a rather different sort of club that originated in Hackney, in London's East End! How times have changed! P & O got rid of the name many years ago, as it was felt it didn't give the right image for the new style of cruising. Too true! Appropriately it was *Chusan* that made the very last P & O line voyage to India, in January 1970. She was retired and scrapped in 1973, just 23 years after her maiden voyage.

P & O was famous for its Goan staff, for whom they had an agreement with the former Portuguese colony of Goa. In the Fifties it featured some of them individually in a series of advertisements. Here's an example, which also gives a 'taste' of P & O's traditional cuisine at that time:

*Caetano X. Fernandes, Table Steward  aboard SS Chusan.*

*As you approach your table in the dining saloon, your appetite surges so sharply that you can't help rubbing your hands in anticipation. Instantly, like some friendly genie of folklore, the quiet man in the white jacket materializes by your chair. No sooner are you seated than you find a napkin in your lap and a menu in your hand. You order. The friendly genie smiles - then almost before you realise that he has left your side, the melon appears complete with sugar and ginger. Next your fillet of sole arrives, grilled with a splash of lemon juice. Then comes your Chateaubriand steak, not quite underdone, but just the way you like it. Meanwhile your butter is replenished, your glass filled, your slightest wish attended to. Never in your life have you had such service, and the quiet man is delighted. For he is Caetano X. Fernandes, Table Steward aboard the P & O's SS Chusan, bound for India and the Far East. One of the 72 Goan waiters on board the ship.... a devoted genie of the dining room. Caetano tells you he loves his job, for it is a traditional part of P & O.*

The Goans were devout Roman Catholics and had a little altar down in their recreation room (see picture). Although the crew were mostly Roman Catholic, on Sundays at sea there was always a Morning Service conducted by the Captain. This basically followed the Church of England's *Book of Common Prayer* - now replaced in most places by one called, unfortunately but appropriately, *Common Worship.* A good number of other officers would accompany the Captain into the First Class Lounge, to which Tourist class passengers would be admitted on this special occasion only, unless there was a cinema on board, when the service would take place there. As the Officers entered, caps under their arms, the congregation would rise as one man - although we would then be told it was OK to remain seated for the prayers! There was always a packed attendance back in those days of the Sixties and Seventies, and we *always* sang "Eternal Father" - the sailors' hymn. My mother used to say she remembered the Salvation Army band playing it on Liverpool Pierhead in times of stormy weather! The lesson (usually only one!) would often be read by one of the attractive young Hostesses, which cheered up the gentlemen. Afterwards there would be a collection at the door for Seamen's charities.  If one was lucky, one might then be invited up to the Ward Room, where the Officers would have

Sunday morning drinks. This was referred to, rather coyly, as a 'Ward Room Meeting!'

My first sight of *Chusan* in Venice has remained an indelible memory throughout my life. Unlike modern Butlins-on-Sea monsters, which must berth way out where they disgorge their thousands, Chusan was small enough (and port regulations still flexible enough) to permit her to tie up close to San Marco, and thus become, for a day or two, an integral part of city life. Small she may have been by modern standards, but picture how she towered above the churches and hotels of the Riva Schiavoni, reminding passers-by how profound co-existence can be between the beauty of the new and the old. And her smart officers coming ashore in their tropical white uniforms did nothing to detract from the magic of the scene! She was known as 'The Happy Ship', and lived up to her reputation for me and many others.

*Chusan* moored in Venice

# 9

# A Favourite Ship and a Favourite Port

I was extremely fortunate to be appointed to that particular cruise, since - unbeknown to me at the time - the travel writer Eric Newby, who was also Editor of *The Observer* newspaper's travel pages, was a guest on board. His son had been a contemporary of mine at my old school in Hammersmith and I got a very nice write-up in his travel columns in the *Observer*:

" Our lecturer was a young master from Harrow who filled us up with information about what to do and where to go….."

This unexpected and favourable publicity did me no harm at all and no doubt helped to ensure for me a regular slot each summer in the P & O Line's lovely old-fashioned ships, accommodated always at that time in First Class. Those were the days! Some people in First Class used to make horribly patronizing remarks about the lesser mortals (twice as many of them in half as much deck space as us) down aft in Tourist Class: " Of course, my dear, they have much more FUN down there" and so on. But I couldn't see why people would pay quite a lot of money, even in Tourist Class, only to be made to feel inferior and to be reminded of their inferior status at every sight of the 'No Admittance - First Class passengers only' signs! Of course, it was this that eventually did for the two class ships (except for Cunard, who continue to operate their separate 'Grill' class –even down to its own sub-divisions- Princess or Queen's Grill.) With increasing affluence and desire for foreign travel in the Sixties and Seventies, the shipping lines found they could fill First Class, but not Tourist. And passengers were increasingly openly rebellious about staying in their own sections of the ship.

***Chusan****: Goans' Chapel*

When I came to give my first lecture in *Chusan* on Lisbon I dwelt on Portugal's great imperial past and her links with Britain, reminding the audience that Portugal was Britain's oldest ally, by the Treaty of Windsor of 1386 - the world's oldest recorded alliance. To say nothing of the historic Port Wine Treaty of 1703 and Britain's intervention in the early nineteenth century Peninsular War! Our King Charles II's long-suffering wife, Catherine of Braganza, came from the North East corner of Portugal. Although Portugal's Prime Minister Salazar was a dictator, he was careful to maintain a strict neutrality for his country throughout the Second World War, and he remained loyal to the Treaty of Windsor. Lisbon became a great centre for espionage during those war years. Anyone who has seen that marvellous movie *Casablanca* starring Humphrey Bogart and Ingrid Bergman, will remember the heart-tugging finale, when the plane carrying the refugee Victor Lazlo leaves for Lisbon and freedom, just as the occupying Nazis arrive at the airport to arrest him. And it was during those years in wartime Lisbon that James Bond was born in the mind of his creator. Ian Fleming was based in the Estoril Palace Hotel on a diplomatic mission. There were also several crowned but displaced Heads of European states living in or near Estoril at the time - including the former Kings of Italy and Rumania, the former Regent of Hungary, Admiral Horthy, and three Pretenders: Don Juan, the claimant to the Spanish throne, and father of former King Juan Carlos, the Comte de Paris, Pretender to the throne of France, and the Archduke Joseph Francis of Hapsburg!

After the end of the war, the women of Portugal paid to erect the great statue of Christ on the banks of the Tagus, which now stands next to the Bridge of the 25th April facing the city. It's an echo of the famous statue in Rio de Janeiro (a former Portuguese city, of course) and was given in thanksgiving that their men had not been involved directly in the war.

After my Lisbon lecture had finished, I was touched to be thanked fulsomely by a group of Portuguese passengers, who had been moved by my emphasis on the bonds between our two countries. I was pleased I had avoided any disparaging remarks about Portugal's current politics!

One of the features of Lisbon that captured me back in those days was the large number of ancient yellow-painted trams plying the narrow steep streets of the city of Seven Hills. They would clang their swaying way along, with frequent ringing of their bells as cars and other vehicles crossed their paths. Often their platforms were commandeered by street urchins to hitch a ride, or, even more perilously, to cling on with one hand, while riding an ancient bicycle! These days the few remaining old trams on Route 28 'the Route of the Hills,' besieged now by tourists, have been fitted with electric doors to keep out the free-riders.

From Lisbon we sailed on down the Portuguese coast, rounding Cape St Vincent:

'Nobly, nobly Cape Saint Vincent to the North-West died away;
Sunset ran, one glorious blood-red, reeking into Cadiz Bay;
Bluish 'mid the burning water, full in face Trafalgar lay;
In the dimmest North-East distance, dawned Gibraltar grand and gray.'

Those lines, from Robert Browning's 'Home thoughts From the Sea,' still haunt me as one passes the Cape, and, even more, as one approaches the great Rock of Gibraltar, one of the last remaining outposts of the old British Empire. In the 1960s it was still a relatively workaday sort of place, heavily dependent on its naval dockyard. Tourist facilities were sparse: the old Rock Hotel, with its colonial atmosphere, was the grand place to go for tea (like Reid's in Madeira), but the real point of calling at the Rock (unless you enjoyed the antics of the famous apes, a tail-less breed of monkey, who inhabit the upper reaches of the Rock) was Duty Free! Main

Street was crowded with off-licences and tobacconists, all vying with each other to quote the lowest price and offer to

*The Rock of Gibraltar (P & O Poster)*

deliver your parcels and boxes to the ship. Sadly, nowadays many of the mass market cruise ships demand their passengers give up their duty-free bottles at the gangway until the end of the cruise, in an effort to maintain their income from bar sales aboard!

At the far end of Main Street, walking along it from the docks and Casemates Square, one reaches the Trafalgar cemetery. Many of Nelson's sailors, killed along with the great Admiral at the Battle of Trafalgar, lie in this peaceful green square. Nelson's own body was shipped back to England, preserved in a barrel of Navy rum, for burial in St Paul's Cathedral. But when the barrel was opened there was no rum - it appears the ratings had drunk it all!

*Artificial 'Dolphins' in the Gibraltar pool*

A popular ship's excursion from Gibraltar was, and still is, to go out into the Straits in a small boat to view the dolphins, sporting out at sea. Since, in those pre-internet days, one was mainly dependent upon one's own collection of slides to illustrate lectures, I thought to take my camera out to sea on the trip, in order to get some good pictures of the dolphins to promote the tour on our next visit. But the dolphins proved very elusive. Not one! By the time I had focused on them as they leapt around the boat they were away, to my intense frustration. Not to be thwarted, I hit on a novel plan. I knew that at the public outdoor swimming pool, along the Gibraltar waterfront, there were some concrete statues of Dolphins! So I carefully photographed them (see photo!) and for many years I tried to pass them off in my talks as the real McCoy! Or at least an apology for them!

From Gibraltar we steamed across the Med to Naples, where the intense, rowdy life of the old Spaccanapoli Quarter thrilled me, along with the grandeur of its many baroque palaces and churches. Along the waterfront in the Santa Lucia quarter the local boys – i ragazzi - still dived for coins from the tourists, or posed on the rocks, like models in photographs by wicked old Baron von Gloeden down in Taormina at the turn of the nineteenth century.

*Naples: Castel del Ovo and Santa Lucia waterfront*

## 10

# When the Going was Good

Cruising was so much more leisurely back in those days in the Sixties. Instead of a frantic dash from port to port, there would be perhaps five ports of call during a two week Mediterranean cruise. And the shore excursions, as they were always called (never 'tours'), were also more leisurely, mostly with elaborate lunches included in good local restaurants. There were even separate tour buses for each class of passenger! In those days these meals ashore made a welcome break from the rather monotonous 'British' or Indian style cuisine on board P & O liners. After a full English breakfast, or a plate of kippers or steamed smoked haddock (both hard to find in modern ships), followed at around 11 by a cup of Bouillon on deck, one would be served a three or four course lunch.

Dinner was always at least four courses, always with a separate fish course. Curry dishes, which came with all the trimmings, were often the best option for the main course, bearing in mind the Line's Indian, or Goan, heritage and crew. The vegetables were usually overcooked! I well remember the passengers' critical comments when P & O tried to modernise their cuisine aboard the new *Oriana*. A top chef from the Dorchester Hotel was engaged to advise and plan the menus, but the old-style passengers complained bitterly of, "Half-cooked vegetables!"

If we were in port for the evening, or overnight (and that was much more frequent in the old days!) the Entertainment staff liked to go for a meal ashore, in the company of some of the younger officers. I was invited to join such a group in Lisbon by Celia, the First Class Social Hostess. She made it very clear to me that being invited to join Officers was a great honour and one was supposed to pay the bill for them! The favourite place to go in Lisbon was (and still is, as far as I know) the *Bomjardim*, a bustling Portuguese restaurant in a very lively street in the Baixa district. It specialises in chicken and chips! On our return to the ship it began to dawn on me, innocent as I was in those far-off days, that I might be expected to accompany the First Class Social Hostess back into her cabin! I fled and Celia cut me dead thereafter, except when she had to introduce me at a lecture!

On another occasion, when our ship was anchored in the lovely bay between Cap Ferrat and Cap de Nice off the picturesque little port of Villefranche, I ventured ashore with a party containing the ship's Doctor. As dinner ashore dragged on I became increasingly anxious about catching the last tender back on board. "No need to worry, old boy," the well-oiled Doctor assured me, "It's against maritime regulations for a passenger ship to sail without a Doctor!" I might add that ship's doctors in those days tended to be rather red-faced old soaks, who, one suspected, were really there for the beer (or rather the wine and spirits)! I gathered ships' doctors were allowed to keep the fees they charged passengers on board, presumably in lieu of salary. That could have been a very lucrative arrangement with some of the more valetudinarian passengers! There were certain ones who were notorious for spending the greater part of their cruise in the ship's hospital, where they could be waited on, hand and foot. Useful if you had only paid for Tourist class and didn't want to go ashore! Of course, ships' doctors are no longer paid in that way and they seem to be increasingly young, and usually foreign, these days.

Travelling as I was by myself, I was glad of the companionship of fellow 'Entertainers.' I remember particularly Vicki Anderson, a British cabaret and jazz singer, with whom I had the good fortune to be seated in *Chusan*'s First Class Restaurant. In those days, and even today in some traditional style ships, one was allocated a place for all meals for the whole cruise in the appropriate restaurant for one's cabin class. The table seating was arranged by the Chief Steward, who took considerable care over the seating plans to ensure, as far as possible, compatible and agreeable neighbours. This did not prevent an anxious queue of passengers forming at his table just inside the restaurant in the afternoon of Embarkation Day with requests for a change of place or sitting. There were two sittings for dinner at around 6.30pm and 8.30pm. One heard stories of brash Cockney types producing a £20 note and tearing it in half in front of the Head Waiter, while exclaiming, "You'll get the other 'alf if everything is good!" I never descended to such a level myself, but I do recall handing £20 to the Head Steward in *QE2*'s *Caronia* Restaurant to ensure my companion and I could be seated with another friend and his partner. It worked!

Anyway, Vicki took me under her wing in the nicest possible way to show me the ropes. Amongst other little bits of ship's etiquette, she showed me how to reward the stewards who served our drinks. Regular passengers still paid cash on board and thus were able to round up sums, by way of a tip. We entertainers had the privilege of signing chits for drinks, along with the ship's Officers, in those days when cash was still king aboard ship. We paid at the end of the cruise at heavily discounted prices. So, in order to reward the stewards, it was the custom to ask them what they would have. They usually replied, "Slops, please, Sir" which was an Allsops lager from Australia. One added that to the chit with one's own order. Of course, they couldn't consume it there and then, but it was no doubt credited to them in some way- possibly down in the crew bar, usually known as the 'Pig and

Whistle.' Towards the end of the cruise, one was sometimes invited down there for a few drinks by a friendly crew member, especially if the crew were putting on some kind of entertainment themselves.

It was rumoured that some of the shadier passengers paid for their whole cruise in cash! Hence the presence on board of undercover officials from the Inland Revenue, who were there to check on the big spenders! This also explained why we were always asked if we wished our names to be included in the little booklets of passengers' names and their home towns that were distributed to guests. Likewise, the ship's photographers were cautious about photographing couples, in case the resulting picture might later be produced in the Divorce Court, or sent to the Inland Revenue by a jilted partner.

Another, very different cabaret performer was Manuela. It was her first contract at sea and she was very nervous. I'm afraid some of us used to wind her up unmercifully. She brought a lot of this on herself, never appearing on deck without full make-up and an enormous 'beehive' hairdo, which it was rumoured was actually a wig. More Danny La Rue than Spanish! Actually she came from plain old Acton in West London, we discovered. (But then, so did Adam Faith!) Manuela was terrified that she might be attacked by randy stewards: she never opened her cabin door without hooking it up, so it only opened a few inches. These hooks had been a device in use before air conditioning, when it was the only way to get a current of air through the cabin. Air conditioning had been installed in all P & O's passenger liners by the mid Sixties, but the hook and eye arrangement remained on the cabin doors.

Mostly I had congenial table companions in the P & O ships, but I recall one difficult table. To break the ice on our first night I offered to buy the wine for our table of four. This was accepted with alacrity by my three companions. When the wine steward appeared on the next night they looked at me expectantly. I averted my eyes but no offer was forthcoming. Eventually the man opposite broke the silence with," You get it free, don't you?" "Officers do get an allowance to buy the wine for their table," I explained, "but I'm afraid I don't fall into that category." So no wine at dinner that night! I was tempted to add that they were not in the category of passengers who might be invited to one of the senior officers' tables! It was always a matter of pride for some passengers to be invited to the Captain's table, but there's a corny joke that does the rounds. A very brash new passenger, on finding he was to be seated at the Captain's table, exclaimed indignantly, "I haven't paid all this money to be seated with the staff!"

It was rumoured that the ship's Head Bartenders were amongst the wealthiest persons on board, since, when cash was king, all manner of 'fiddles' were possible! It was common for an unscrupulous barman to water down the spirits he served to passengers. Junior officers often carried little devices that measured the specific gravity of spirits, to check if they had been diluted by the bar staff.

Only once, as a young man travelling alone, did an older steward attempt an indiscretion. It was in the *Himalaya* and I had one of the former First Class cabins, although it was by then a one-class vessel. My cabin steward came in to turn down the bed and tidy the cabin for the night, as was usual, while I was in the bathroom. I thought nothing of this and anyway needed to get dressed for dinner. (In those distant days it was the custom - even in a one class Tourist Class ship! - to dress formally in Black Tie for dinner on every Sea Day, except the first and last nights.) So I wrapped my bath towel around myself and came out of the bathroom to put a dress shirt on. At that point I felt the cabin steward's hand resting on my back. I said nothing and merely removed it. And nothing more occurred or was said. Had I reported the matter the poor man might have lost his job.

My mother subsequently told me that, when she was having trouble zipping up the back of her evening dress, she had called for a stewardess (there were always a few such, on call for such eventualities, in an otherwise all male crew), but her cabin steward appeared and offered to zip her up himself! I'm not sure if he was the same one as mine, but, anyway, his offer was politely declined and I was sent for in order to perform the vital task! How different it all is in these days of 'Me Too!'

*The Second **Oriana** in Sydney in her Orient Line livery*

August 1974 saw me lecturing aboard the old *Oriana,* which was definitely an improvement in many ways on the earlier ships. She had been the flagship of the Orient Line, launched in 1959, and was the fastest ship in the fleet, reaching over 30 knots. She had an interesting design feature, in that cabins in middle price range were arranged in groups of six in 'Courts' that opened off the main interior corridor. The court widened as it reached a large window in the ship's side. The four interior cabins (two on each side) each had an L-shaped plan, so that they overlapped each other, as the 'Court' got wider towards the ship's side. Each of these four interior cabins had a window in the corner fitted with a blind, so they could gain light and a restricted view from the large window at the end of the court. Of course it meant that, if the blind remained pulled up, visitors to the court could also see into those cabins!

Another feature of the old *Oriana* was that she had a two-storey cinema, so that First Class passengers could sit up in the balcony and not be sullied by contact with the lower orders! The low wall in front of the balcony also provided a useful perch for the slide projector! In those days we were provided with a Kodak Carousel projector to project our own slides to illustrate our lectures. As soon as I joined the ship I used to pick up a couple of slide cassettes for the Carousel from the 'Ents' office on board, so I could load them up with slides in the correct order and, hopefully, the right way up! I think each one took about 80 slides, but sometimes I needed a few more in a second cassette. This necessitated a change of cassette, which was tricky when it was perched up on the edge of the balcony. Fortunately, however, my mother was sailing with me and so she volunteered to change the cassettes at the appropriate time. I was a bit nervous about this, as I knew well her propensity to fall asleep during my lectures! So, when I was about to get to the changeover, I said, very loudly, "Cassette change coming up!" and waited for results. There was a sound of fumbling up in the front of the balcony. A fellow lecturer had decided my mother looked as if she needed his 'help.' That, of course, was the last thing she needed, as it flustered her and there was a slightly embarrassing delay. I suspected my fellow lecturer might have deliberately caused this hiatus and this was confirmed when I visited P & O's office after the cruise and was warned that my lectures were 'lacking in humour and polish!' I replied, " Well I've been giving these talks for about ten years and received no complaints." "Perhaps that's the problem," was the reply. Since then I've always been careful to update my material and include some humour! As for the other lecturer, we became friends and have helped each other out many times with slides and port information over the years.

One of the pleasant features of shipboard life in those days was private parties, either informally in one's own cabin, or in the whole 'alley' or Court, if neighbours wanted to join. For larger groups one could book one of the smaller public rooms and arrange for stewards to serve. When I sailed accompanied by my mother, after my father's premature death, I took to giving one of these receptions, so I could invite other entertainers and guests we had met on board. At one of these parties, on board *Oriana,* I had the pleasure of entertaining Violet Carson. She played the flint-faced and gruff moral voice of ITV's 'Coronation Street,' Ena Sharples. Violet proved to be a very gracious lady who played the piano for us, and was as different as possible from her television *persona*!

Another very different distinguished passenger on board *Oriana* was Lt. Gen. Frederick Morgan who, during World War 2, had been given the task of dealing with the German thrust through Spain to Gibraltar. The Germans never got there and Morgan's two divisions were sent to North Africa, while he was directed to plan the invasion of Sardinia. In time, this was in turn abandoned, in favour of the Allied invasion of Sicily (Operation Husky), which took place in

July 1943. As we sailed from Gibraltar I was moved to find the old General sitting on one of the high side decks of the ship as an RAF fly past went overhead above. They were saluting him, having been notified that he was aboard. And the ship, of course, was blaring out *Rule Britannia*!

# 11

# The 'First Lady' of P & O

*SS Canberra*

After about ten years' port lecturing during my summer holidays aboard P & O's older ships, including the two one class ships *"Orcades'* and *'Himalaya,' 'Chusan,' 'Oronsay,' 'Orsova'* and the more modern and larger *Oriana*, I was finally given a chance to graduate in August 1976 to P & O's 'First Lady,' the glamorous flagship *Canberra*. I had eyed her longingly on various occasions as we passed her in Southampton docks. She had beautiful lines, with her pioneering twin stacks to the Aft of the vessel. In later days she was usually berthed at the Ocean Terminal, now demolished. Back in the Fifties and Sixties it had been the grand transatlantic terminal from whence Cunard's 2 Queens - the *Mary* and the *Elizabeth* - regularly sailed on the classic transatlantic run, taking just 4 days to cross the 'Pond.' Nowadays *Queen Mary 2* takes 6 days 'not because she *couldn't*' in the words of that flirtatious song of Marlene Dietrich, '*The Laziest Girl in Town,*' 'not because she *wouldn't*' - but because Carnival Corporation, the new Cunard owners, want to save fuel and get more revenue aboard with an extended time at sea! And I suppose, if 'the Ship is the Destination,' is true it makes sense.

Little did I expect that the glamorous, relatively new *Canberra*, built in Belfast at Harland and Woolf's great shipyard, where the *Titanic* had been built, and launched in 1961 by Dame Pattie Menzies, wife of the Australian Prime Minister, would end her days as a one class cruise ship! And neither did anyone else when she was launched for the Australia run and the emigrant trade. Her design was ambitiously forward-thinking, but unfortunately during her sea trials, a major flaw was discovered. When going at high speed, the bow lifted itself out of the water, because of the weight of the engines aft. To remedy this problem, the ship was sent to Southampton where some of her forward compartments were filled with ballast as counterweight, thus causing her to lie lower in the water, and consequently have a deeper draught than had been planned. At least this avoided the necessity of walking uphill as one progressed through the ship's interior! It also gave her great stability - but at the cost of pushing a load of concrete around the world as she sailed! And her deep draught also limited the ports that could accommodate her. This wasn't a problem on the line voyages for which she had been planned, but it certainly limited her versatility when she turned to cruising. I was on board on one occasion when she ran aground in Southampton Water and we had to wait for the tide to float us off.

Throughout the 1960s there were problems with strikes by militant dockers in *Canberra*'s home port of Southampton. In

1965 it was the turn of the seamen's union to strike over pay and conditions for 45 days. They demanded a shorter working week *and* a 17% pay increase. Since they had already had a 13% increase the previous year, the shipowners refused, and so the docks became full with laid up vessels. P&O had to cancel three of Canberra's cruises. Fortunately the dispute was resolved before her World Cruise and so she was able to sail.

By the end of the Sixties, the emigrant trade was shrinking, with Australia becoming increasingly fussy about whom she let in. And air travel was becoming cheaper and faster with the jet age. This was the writing on the wall for the ocean liner. Fuel costs were soaring and demand falling. So something new was required and P&O decided to send *Canberra* across to New York, where she would be marketed (by Cunard of all companies!) for cruises, mainly to the Caribbean.

This proved to be a disaster- bookings were minimal and, after just 2 cruises, *Canberra* was laid up. The future looked grim. After her remaining cruises were completed it was announced that *Canberra* – just 12 years old - was to be scrapped. She had lost £500,000 between February and September 1972. Somebody should have realised Americans on a 'luxury cruise' would expect their own private bathrooms in *every* cabin!

The situation wasn't helped when *Canberra* went aground again, this time off Grenada. But, while she was still aground, things suddenly took a turn for the better. With the end of the oil crisis, there was a massive surge in cruise bookings. P & O announced (after a Board Room revolt) that they would no longer be selling her. Instead, she would take the place of *Orsova* in her 1974 cruising programme. *Canberra* was refloated with the aid of two tugs and continued on her voyage. After completing the rest of her US programme she returned to England where her class barriers were removed for cruising and her capacity reduced to just over 1,700, by converting a number of the old 4 berth emigrant cabins into twins.

*Canberra* had finally found her niche! In 1977, the chairman of P&O announced that the passenger division had made a £4.1 million profit in 1976, as opposed to a loss of £6.9 million in 1975. I had noticed the men from McKinseys, the business efficiency experts, aboard previous to this. It seemed that their medicine was working!

Although things were going well, the price of fuel was still rising rapidly and so engine and propeller changes were made, to reduce fuel consumption. By 1981 P & O's British passenger ships consisted solely of *Canberra*! Then came another surprising turn in *Canberra's* fortunes. She was called into service in the Falklands War in April 1982. She was fitted with two helicopter decks and made ready to receive her new passengers: British soldiers. *Canberra* was transformed from a cruise ship to a warship in just three days! That was the only year P & O ever cancelled my booking as Port Lecturer! But *Canberra* was back in her old role in September 1982 and continued sailing from Southampton or Sydney.

So *Canberra* became famous as the 'Falklands Ship,' after her heroic service in the South Atlantic. After having brought troops and equipment down to the Falklands, in company with *QE2* and the old British India school cruise ship *Uganda*, which became a hospital ship, Canberra stayed on in San Carlos Water, off Port Stanley, the islands' capital. She was a sitting duck target ('The Great White Whale,' she was called) during many bombing raids over some weeks, but miraculously she survived intact. After her triumphant return, her fame and popularity was such that P & O actually

*Canberra's triumphant return from the Falklands*

changed their name for a few years to *"Canberra* cruises!' I still have a tie inscribed with that name, to prove it!

My heart had been in my mouth throughout the Falklands War, not only in trepidation for the fate of the British forces, but also for the loyal crew of the *Canberra,* all 900 of whom had volunteered to sail South with their ship, although only 400 were needed. To say nothing of the 'Old Girl' herself! And who could ever forget that wonderful triumphant sail up Southampton Water, with the old lady rust-stained but unbowed, crowded with the jubilant returning Marines. And the dockside was packed with family members and loved ones. A large colour photograph of that return had pride of place in the ship, on the Aft staircase, until her last days.

QE2 quickly returned to regular service and *Uganda* (for which I had only recently been interviewed for the post of Deputy Head!) remained down in the South Atlantic for some time, as a hospital ship. *Canberra* eventually returned, after transporting large numbers of captured young Argentine soldiers back to their native land. I met some of them later on a beach in Ibiza. They were mere boys, and many of their comrades in arms had been drowned when Margaret Thatcher gave the order to sink the ancient Argentinian troopship the *Belgrano*, even though it was steaming away from the Exclusion Zone at that time. I could understand why she felt she couldn't take a risk with it, at the possible expense of our own troops, but it was a dreadful decision to have to take and I've never forgotten the gloatingly triumphant headline the next day in the *Sun* newspaper: "GOTCHA!" which sadly thrilled my then Headmaster!

A year or two after her service down in the Falklands, I was on board when *Canberra* docked in Vigo in North West Spain. Load banging noises echoed inside the ship. On investigating further up on deck, I saw a group of men on the quayside hurling stones and other objects at our hull. Truly we were the 'Falklands Ship' and the Galicians regarded us with hostility, since many of their kinsfolk had emigrated to Argentina and there were still strong links between Galicia, with its history of emigration, and Argentina! Furthermore, Generalissimo Franco, still Caudillo of Spain, was a Galician and was busy blockading Gibraltar around that time! So we were doubly unpopular.

By the end of the eighties, *Canberra* was beginning to show her age, developing (minor) mechanical troubles. I well remember one occasion. We had just sailed from Naples and settled down to the usual P & O four-course dinner when the lights went out in the Restaurant and the emergency ones came on. After a short delay the Captain's voice came over the Tannoy to say we had experienced a loss of power and we were asked gather on deck, since the Restaurant was beginning to get rather warm without the air conditioning functioning. So there we were, all dressed up for dinner, up on deck and adrift in the crowded Bay of Naples! Fortunately power was restored after an hour or so and we all trooped back downstairs to face the cold remains of dinner!

In 1992 P & O ordered a new cruise ship of around 67.000 tons from Meyer Werft in Germany and the writing was on the wall for *Canberra*. Finally, on June 25th 1996, P&O announced that *Canberra* would be retired from service on September 30th 1997. She would be withdrawn just before the introduction of new safety rules.

Her capacious Sports arena up forward had been converted into a makeshift theatre for shows, with uncomfortable upright chairs, dreadful sightlines and very rudimentary air conditioning machines. A primitive self-service buffet had also been installed on the after-deck for lunch. It reminded one of a school canteen! But this was all part of the decision to go one-class in a ship which very obviously had been built for two classes! And at least it saved the ship!

After the conversion of *Canberra* to one-class cruising, lecturers were in for a nasty shock. We had been used to occupying luxurious First Class accommodation in return for our (unpaid) services and so dining in the First Class Pacific Restaurant. Lectures were organized in separate sittings in the ship's cinema for each class.

Two thirds of the ship's accommodation had been allotted to the approximately one third of passengers who travelled First (and paid accordingly!). In those days, deck buffet lunches were an occasional treat in First Class, but never in Tourist Class! I'm always amused when people reminisce about the happy times they spent aboard *Canberra* in those halcyon days of yore, before ships became one class palaces. Unless *all* these folk sailed First Class, they have forgotten the primitive conditions in the Tourist section of the ship. Around two thirds of the cabins (even in *Canberra*) were without private facilities, which meant using the common bathrooms and the communal Ladies or Gents' lavatory blocks. During the not infrequent bouts of dysentery - jokingly referred to by one Captain I remember as the "*Canberra* bug' - stewards were employed to standby in the 'Heads' to wipe down the lavatory handles, seats and door handles with disinfectant during such bouts. This was before we knew about 'Norovirus' of course, although the symptons were just the same! As we returned to the ship from a shore excursion one droll fellow passenger suggested that *Canberra* should be flying the signal that denoted there was plague on board! Little did one expect that in 2020 cruise ships would find themselves in exactly that position, banned from ports because of Covid-19 cases on board!

We were due to call at Naples during an outbreak of typhoid fever in the city, which had allegedly originated in the fish restaurants of the Santa Lucia district, down on the waterfront. Mussels, served up in Spaghetti al Vongole and other dishes, were named as the probable source of infection. The port authorities took the drastic step of blowing up the off-shore mussel beds with depth charges, thus destroying the local fishermen's livelihood. When I saw the Naples ferry entering Palermo harbour it conjured up vivid images of people escaping from plagues in Oran in Camus's novel 'The Plague' or Venice in Mann's 'Death in Venice" as passengers streamed off. I never expected to be writing this while we are all trying to escape from a more deadly plague!

By 1974 there had already been a downward progression (or regression, perhaps) in lecturers' accommodation from A

71

Deck Forward to D deck mid-ships. But, in a one-class ship, the bottom was literally the limit! The next summer I found myself occupying a former '£10 Pom' Australian emigrants' cabin down in the bowels of G deck aft! Thankfully, one pair of bunks had been removed to permit the installation of a shower and lavatory, leaving the other pair of bunks- one up and one down. We were below the water-line in what the Company had coyly named 'Equity Court,' but which some of us renamed 'Jacques Cousteau Court!' after the famous French diver. The engines throbbed somewhere close by and I felt pretty hard done-by, until I came across the boys and girls of the Chorus, also accommodated down below in Equity Court, who were queuing to use the common showers after their exhausting twice nightly shows!

The ship's Chaplain was also billeted in the same Court and complained that he had the rushing sea on one side of his cabin and the harpist and his athletic girl friend humping all night on the other side! After these revelations I felt privileged, and indeed embarrassed, to be the only one on G deck Aft to have my own shower and loo! There was one compensation. *Canberra* was a remarkably stable ship, partly due to the large amount of ballast she had to carry to keep her prow down after her design fault emerged. However, on the night we sailed from Southampton in a Force 9 gale, I was very glad to be down on G Deck Aft - the most stable location in the ship!

The last night of a cruise was always a bit wild, especially in *Canberra* in the old days. Some of the rougher element – those who paid their fares for the cruise in cash - would drink themselves silly into the early hours. I don't know if the notorious Kray brothers, who ruled London's gangland with a rod of iron in the Fifties and Sixties ever cruised, but some of the entertainers they mixed with in their West End nightclub certainly did, like Barbara Windsor. I was told by a younger actor friend who sailed with me in *Canberra* and enjoyed staying up on the last night that I was described by one of the rougher sort as P & O's answer to Julian Clary! At least Clary was nearly 20 years younger than me!

Prior to the late Seventies, and *Canberra*'s conversion to one-class cruising, entertainment on board P and O ships had been mostly homespun. No chorus girls or boys (unless you counted some of the crew in a drag show!) and just one comedian or, if you were very lucky, a magician.

The 'Race Night' was a high point of each cruise. A number of ladies were appointed 'jockeys' and given a primitive spool, which pulled a cut-out 'horse' along a fixed track. There was much martial music and strutting around by gentlemen placing bets on likely 'fillies.' The money remaining after the prizes had been paid went to ships' charities. On other nights there would be a fancy dress party, or some amateur entertainment, if anyone thought they could sing or play the piano. A children's fancy dress party was usually an early evening highlight, when they would be led forth, some winningly shy, others more boisterous, from the large and well staffed children's area. Then there was the crew's own show, which often featured some of the likely lads in drag. I heard later that such antics were stopped by Lord Sterling, when he became Chairman of P and O, after the Anderson family and their company, headed by the Earl of Inchcape, sold out.

Sterling, who was an accountant by profession, had, I gathered, headed off an earlier bid by the Bovis construction company, of all unlikely bidders! I believe he was later instrumental in persuading the company to invest in the new liner, the third *Oriana,* to be built by Meyer Werft in Germany. A special point was made that she must be fast enough to get down to the Med, and back, at a fair speed, catering for her British clientele on their (most commonly) two week cruises to the sun and for her annual world cruise in the early part of each year. Like her predecessor, she was capable of 30 knots and remained the fastest ship in the fleet, until P & O retired her in 2019. Most current cruise ships are only capable of steaming at around 20 knots, if one is lucky! Hence the prevalence today of 'fly cruising,' where one flies down, usually to the Med, to join the ship in sunnier climes.

P & O had already made a few attempts to break into that market, basing an older, smaller ship, like little *Chitral,* down in Genoa or a similar Mediterranean port, for the summer. But it never really took off for P & O. Many of their clientele didn't care to fly, and they enjoyed the two or three day sail down to warmer waters while they relaxed on board and I, or someone else, lectured on the pleasurable ports ahead! Later on, companies like Thomson (now TUI) were able to make a success of fly cruising, using refurbished old ships, like Holland America's former *Nordam.* Thomson were already well known in the package tour industry and were able to persuade their rather different clientele to take to the sea as a development of a package holiday.

In addition to the homespun ('shipspun?') entertainment, there were also one or two slightly faded singing stars, who, like me, were formerly accommodated in First Class, in exchange for their services. I well remember dear Joan Regan, who had been a big television star and was travelling with her husband, a Doctor, in a cabin just along our alley up front in the old *Oriana.* She had become rather shortsighted, but didn't wear her glasses or contact lenses when she was on stage. She was liable, therefore, to address sentimental love songs to quite the wrong persons in the room!

s.s. "Oronsay"  Race Card

# MEDITERRANEAN SEA
# RACE MEETING

To be held on "Oronsay" Race Course,
Saturday, 11th August, 1962

*Patron :*
Captain S. Ayles, R.D., R.N.R.

*Judges :*
Air Vice Marshall R. A. Ramsey-Rae, C.B., O.B.E.
Mr. W. H. Williamson

| *Starter :* | *Timekeeper :* |
| --- | --- |
| Mr. P. Pierson | Mr. A. C. Williams |

*The Tote will open at 9-15 p.m.*
*Tickets 1/- each.     Any number may be taken*

(10 per cent will be deducted for Marine Charities)
*There will be a Tote Double on the 3rd and 5th Races*

**FIRST RACE 9-30 p.m.**

---

# RULES

1. The winning horse in each race will run in the final.

2. In the event of a dead-heat only the horses concerned will race again.

3. One beat on the gong will be sounded four minutes before the start of each race, and two beats two minutes before the start, when the Tote will close.

4. The Judges' decision is final.

# PROGRAMME OF RACES

| 1st Race | THE SINGAPORE STAKES | 9-30 p.m. |
|---|---|---|
| Nominator | Horse and Pedigree | Jockey |
| 1. Mr. J. H. Lund | HIRE PURCHASE<br>By Husband out of Money | Mrs. Lund |
| 2. Mr. K. W. Walker | BARE BACK<br>By Tortoise out of Shell | Mrs. Walker |
| 3. Mr. T. de B. H. Stride | EMBARRASSMENT<br>By Slip out of Place | Mrs. Stride |
| 4. Mr. S. A. H. Carpenter | WIND UP<br>By Scared out of Wits | Mrs. Carpenter |
| 5. Mr. J. T. Reid | SUN TAN<br>By Protection out of Sunburn | Mrs. Reid |

| 2nd Race | THE COLOMBO CANTER | 9-45 p.m. |
|---|---|---|
| 1. Mr. S. Vasey | SAFETY PIN<br>By Suspender out of Action | Mrs. Vasey |
| 2. Mr. E. R. Quince | HOLY SMOKE<br>By Bishop out of Temper | Miss L. Quince |
| 3. Mr. G. Sloan | OLD STORY<br>By Motor Car out of Petrol | Miss V. Buckle |
| 4. Mr. T. C. Hutchison | STUNG<br>By Bee out of Hive | Mrs. Hutchison |
| 5. Air Vice Marshall<br>R. A. Ramsey-Rae] | DISCORD<br>By Piano out of Tune | Mrs. Ramsey-Rae |

| 3rd Race | THE ADEN AMBLE | 10 p.m. |
|---|---|---|
| 1. Mr. S. Pethick | FAUX PAS<br>By Remark out of Place | Mrs. Pethick |
| 2. Mr. J. L. Snowball | FLYING FISH<br>By Wings out of Sea | Mrs. Snowball |
| 3. Mr. W. M. Thomson | ORONSAY<br>By Vickers out of Barrow | Mrs. Thomson |
| 4. Mr. H. Stafford | BLONDIE<br>By Bleach out of Bottle | Mrs. J. Kitson |
| 5. Mr. I. G. Lakin | CHASTE LADY<br>By Wolf out of Breath | ~~Mrs. S. Burke~~ |

*Race Card for Meeting aboard P & O **Oronsay** 1962*

# 12

# A New Broom

By 1984 the future of P & O as a shipping line, rather than a
mere ferry operator, was looking pretty bleak. *Canberra* was
now their only British-based passenger ship and she had
always had that design fault which necessitated her carrying
extra ballast to compensate for her prow's tendency to rise.
This made her a relatively expensive ship to operate, in spite
of her sleek modern styling. Her twin funnels at the rear of
the ship meant the First Class pool and Bonito Club adjoining
were fairly free of smuts, although the poor old Tourists at
the after end still risked being covered with smuts if the wind
was in that direction, since their pool and most of their deck
space was aft. She also had a propensity to go aground,
because of her deep draught.

Back in 1973, P&O had announced that *Canberra* was to be
withdrawn from service, largely because her deep draught
prevented her from berthing at many popular cruise
ports. *Orsova* was to be rebuilt as a cruise ship and sail in
tandem with *Oriana*. Many P&O directors were appalled that
their flagship might be scrapped (P&O never sold ships for
further service) and that the fleet would consist solely of ex-
Orient ships. After a boardroom battle, the decision was
reversed and *Orsova* was instead withdrawn from service at
the end of 1973. *Canberra* was reprieved, thanks in large part
to strenuous efforts by one of the Company's Directors, who
admired her greatly and had a vision to make her pay.

P & O had taken the Orient Line, with its smart ships with
their corn-coloured hulls, under its wing back in the
Twenties, but had kept the tradition of giving them all names
beginning with 'Or,' as in *Orion, Orcades, Oronsay, Orsova*

and Oriana. The two lines eventually merged fully in 1966 and the former Orient ships were repainted white, like the other P & O ships.

*Orsova* had been built in 1953 and had First and Tourist Class sections, with separate dining rooms either side of the Galley. She was among the first ocean liners to be fitted with air-conditioning. This was installed in the more expensive First-Class cabins, and in the First-Class dining room and lounge. The thermostats in the public rooms, even as the ship crossed the Equator, were kept at 65 deg.F. A tragic side effect of this was that three of the First-Class stewards, running back and forth between the frigid <u>dining room and the un-air-conditioned galley,</u> succumbed to pneumonia and were buried at sea

*Oriana* herself, the fastest ship in the fleet, was put on to full time cruising from 1973 and was moved down to Australia in 1981, where she carried on sailing until she was sold in 1986. It was a P & O practice to send its older ships down to do service as cruise ships based in Australia. This, I was informed, was because Australians usually got drunk, threw furniture overboard and generally trashed the ships!!

But age and high running costs eventually caught up with *Canberra.* She had much higher fuel consumption than more modern cruise ships and, after the fuel crisis of the early Seventies, this mattered increasingly. Although Premier Cruise Line had made a bid for her, P&O had already decided that they did not want *Canberra* to operate under a different flag. *Canberra* was eventually withdrawn from service in September 1997

Lord Sterling of Plaistow had joined the board of P & O as a non-executive director in 1980 and he became Chairman in 1983. Once I witnessed His Lordship being piped aboard by the crew in their impressive native dress! Just like a member of the Royal Family! He had recently been ennobled by Margaret Thatcher, after large donations from his company to the Conservative Party! Later, an item appeared in the papers to say that he had been caught travelling without a ticket on a Southern Region train! 'Shome mishtake shurely!' as *Private Eye's* Lord Gnome would have put it!

When the new *Oriana* had sailed close by and towered over us in dear old *Canberra*, in a kind of naval 'salute,' we had been informed that Lord Sterling was aboard the new vessel. I discovered some years later, when I sailed in that ship with his Lordship aboard, that he had a large area of the after-deck (by then P & O ships were all one class) roped off for the private use of himself and his wife and daughter. One might have thought he was the ship's owner, but he was, of course, only the Company Chairman! But clearly he had a great love of ships and cruising!

On another earlier occasion I encountered Lord Sterling and his party on a lower deck in the *Victoria*, formerly the *Sea Princess* (and originally the *Kungsholm* of the Swedish America Line before P & O bought her) "Oh," inquired his lordship, passing through on his way to the ship's lower exit, "Is this where they keep you?" I wanted to reply, " Yes, along with the performing monkeys," but my courage failed me. Anyway, he might have thought I was referring disparagingly to the Goan crew! (Entertainers and Lecturers had already begun their downward and aft-ward progress through the now one class ships. I had started on the then *Sea Princess's* A Deck and got down to D deck, which was the lowest passenger deck. Entertainers were accommodated close to the Beauty Salon down there, which wasn't much use to me! There was always a strong smell of diesel oil down there as well, not masked by the various beauty products!)

Having changed the name of their British cruising operation to '*Canberra* Cruises,' P & O had to change their name back when times improved under Lord Sterling and new ships began to be acquired or built. First, in 1995, came the new *Oriana*, at the Meyer-Werft yard in Germany; then, five years later, her sister ship *Aurora*. Under the auspices of America's Carnival Corporation, have come the monsters of today, like *Iona*, catering for up to 5,200 passengers! A far cry indeed from *Chusan*, with her 464 first class passenger capacity and 541 Tourist class!

*Arcadia (Formerly **Star Princess**, then **Ocean Village**, etc,etc)*

# *13*

## A change of ship and a change of company

When the time finally came for *Canberra's* retirement in 1997, P & O moved the former *Star Princess* from their Princess Cruises division to join the new *Oriana* in their British cruise division. She was renamed *Arcadia,* following the previous *Arcadia,* the selfsame ship in which my friend Nick's girl friend had served back in the Sixties and on which I had met John Batterbee and 'made my number' (as they say in naval Ward Rooms) as a potential Port Lecturer.

This new *Arcadia* was a very different ship from her distinguished predecessor on the Australia run. In fact, she proved to be just a stopgap until the new *Oriana*'s sister ship *Aurora* was built. For a start, unlike any proper P & O ship, she had been built in France in the Chantiers d'Atlantique yard in St Nazaire. She had been ordered by the Italian Sitmar line - the Societa Italiana Trasport Marittimi - the line that P & O took over in 1988. I had met some of its charming Italian officers aboard *Canberra* after the takeover. That had led to my unfortunate comparison of the Naples dock area to Wapping in my talk on the Italians' home port, which had caused my being hauled up before the Captain, after passengers from Wapping had complained! I had been trying to warn passengers of petty crime in the port area.

*Arcadia,* as she was to become in her third, but far from last incarnation, had been launched and named *Sitmar Fair Majesty,* but she was still being fitted out when Sitmar was taken over. She was subsequently renamed *Star Princess* and began operating for P & O's Princess Cruises in 1989. That continued until 1997, when she became *Arcadia.*

I had high hopes when I joined her in Southampton as Port Lecturer in summer 1998, after the ageing *Canberra's* departure. At least one would not be consigned to the dubious joys of *Canberra's* Equity Court! And so it proved. I was assigned a large cabin on A Deck Forward. My joy was short-lived, however, when I entered it and found a large gloomy space! It was the furthest forward cabin on the deck, and that precluded space for a window, or even a porthole. But at least I was no longer sailing below the waterline! That was fine, until we encountered rough seas in the notorious Bay of Biscay. Unless one held on firmly to the furniture one was thrown across the cabin as the ship pitched and rolled! Oh for the stability of G deck in *Canberra!*

*Arcadia* only had one restaurant, well located midships; but, as was also the case in the new *Oriana* with its two restaurants, that was no longer for the likes of the ship's Port Lecturer! I was directed to the Officers Ward Room. That wouldn't have been so bad, had the younger officers who dined there not insisted on having the television on all through dinner. It certainly infuriated the 'Commander,' who was a fellow lecturer and had seen service in the Royal Navy, where there were 'Standards' in the Officers' Ward Room! He complained vociferously, but to little effect. Like me, he had been used to *Victoria* and its pleasant passenger Restaurant. Some time later, I met the Commander ashore, when he was attending a lecture at Rewley House, the Continuing Education Department of Oxford University. I took the opportunity to quiz him about Iceland, since I had perhaps rather rashly accepted an invitation to lecture about it on a forthcoming cruise. The Commander became very conspiratorial in his manner: " Ahem…can't talk much about that, old boy - top security!" I wondered whether he had ever been there at all…

In 2003, after just six years, *Arcadia* was transferred yet again. P&O had decided they needed to shake off their rather 'fuddy-duddy' reputation with a new brand of cruises aimed at young people and families. To cater for them, *Arcadia* was renamed *Ocean Village*. She was repainted in an extraordinary livery featuring a vivid purple, yellow and red swoosh on the bow! Her new name also caused some confusion, since it was also the name of a residential and retail development on the site of part of the old Southampton docks! After just another five years *Ocean Village* sailed on her final farewell voyage under that name and was transferred down to Australia - the usual home for former P & O ships that the Aussies could be let loose on! That lasted for a further eight years until 2016, when it was announced that the ship would be transferred to Cruise & Maritime Voyages as the *Columbus,* becoming their new flagship. And she has already been demoted from those heady heights by the arrival of a newer ship, the *Amy Johnson,* yet another former Carnival ship!

P & O's newly (1995) built *Oriana* (the third of that name) was quite a different proposition. Although her hull was rather boxy, like *Arcadia's,* she had an elegant interior, complete with an atrium, a first for P & O. There was a beautiful library with furniture designed by Lord Snowdon, son of the late Princess Margaret and her husband Tony Armstrong-Jones, the first Lord Snowdon. Sadly, it seemed to be used mainly as a backdrop for portraits of passengers by the ship's photographer! 'In the warmth and class of an English Library,' was the toe-curling sales line! And the Curzon Room was also an extremely elegant venue for recitals, with its microphones cleverly concealed amidst its beautiful chandeliers. In more populist times, I heard it was turned over to a 'theme' restaurant!

*The new, third **Oriana***

When the much-anticipated *Oriana* finally arrived we lecturers and entertainers all looked forward to a return to civilized accommodation. We couldn't have been more wrong! First, we were told we would no longer be included on the Passenger List, but on the Crew List. We were assured this would make no difference to our status on board. Of course, it made all the difference in the world, and we discovered our new accommodation was down on the crew deck. Two bunks, one above the other, and the most minute bathroom imaginable! Furthermore, it was as far forward as cabins went, so one could hear the banging of the waves on the hull in bad weather. The first time this happened I thought someone had left a door open! Just to one side of the lecturer's cabin was the 'M1'- the main thoroughfare through this busy area. The chorus girls and boys' accommodation was immediately behind the cabin- so one had to endure noise from them at night when they boisterously returned after their second show. The Cruise Director's accommodation was in a quieter area, just across the 'M1.'

I could hardly imagine the *doyen* of Port Lecturers, Frank Jackson and his elegant wife Evelyn, whose P & O pedigree went all the way back to the famous *Straths* in the 1940s, putting up with such accommodation, but I was assured he and Evelyn had indeed occupied the selfsame cabin. I wondered which of them climbed up to the top bunk? I didn't have to wonder for long. Frank and Evelyn used to collect contact addresses of their devoted followers on board and, when they sent out their annual Christmas cards to their fans, they had included a request that they write to Lord Sterling, or so the tale went, to protest at the Jacksons' poor accommodation! Well, whatever the truth of the story, that was the end for the Jacksons. Their services were dispensed with, in spite of their great popularity with older passengers.

Frank always spoke without notes and Evelyn was always with him, to see off tours and welcome them back on the quayside, usually complete with hat and gloves. Rather different from the welcome back one receives in today's Seabourn ships! Most of the ship's company will be lined up and gyrating to a jazz band, while serving drinks to the thirsty returnees! In the early days I believe Frank had actually acted as Excursion Manager as well as Lecturer. He was a mine of information about attractions and transport ashore. But it was annoying for me to hear older passengers bemoaning the absence of the Jacksons, when they found I was to be their Port Lecturer! So tactless!

After their departure from P & O, the Jacksons first joined the *Astor,* then a South African liner, for a year or so, before they accepted an invitation to go down-market to the Fred

Olsen line. I also recall one of their admirers being astonished to discover Evelyn Jackson actually shopping ashore, in Romford of all places! It was assumed by many that they were always at sea. Another lecturer told me about Frank's wonderful study in their home, the walls lined with shelves to accommodate his vast collection of slides. Having calculated recently that my own collection of pictures and lectures covers around 400 ports, I am truly grateful for a computer on which to store them all!

Fred Olsen's ships were all refurbished and lengthened old ones, but at least lecturers were given passenger cabins, as in the former P & O ships. I knew the Jacksons were getting on in years when they joined Fred, but was sad to hear later that Frank had lost his words while giving a talk and had to be flown home. "He must have been 80," I remarked to the fellow Lecturer who told me about this and who knew Frank well. "No," he replied, "He was 90 plus: he'd lied about his age!" Sadly, one can no longer do that, since full passport details are always demanded in advance by cruise lines these days!

I pulled the plug on lecturing for P & O myself in 2002, after 33 years lecturing in their ships. Not only was one now forced to endure the very basic cabin accommodation in the Entertainers' area, low down in the prow of the ship, but one was no longer permitted to dine in the Restaurant! Instead, one was expected to dine in the Officers' Ward Room- but *not* with the ship's Officers! We were now instructed to dine after their early sitting and before the later one! To rub salt into this wound, we were also instructed not to enter in the usual way, through their lounge and bar area, but via a tortuous route through the ship's galley stores! After one had picked one's way past various hanging sides of beef and so on, one's appetite had lost some of its edge by the time one reached the back door of the Ward Room!

By then P & O had decided that it was part of the Port Lecturer's remit to push the tours - particularly those that weren't being booked, often for good reasons in my view! I was actually given lists of the tours that needed pushing! My approach as a Port Lecturer has always been to help both passengers who wanted advice to explore ashore by themselves, as well as those who wanted advice about the tours. I certainly wasn't prepared to recommend duff tours.

But the final straw for me was when the Tours Manager observed that, since my lectures had now all been given, I could occupy myself stuffing envelopes in the back office with the tour tickets for the next cruise! They would then be ready for delivery to the next lot of passengers! In other words, I was to be an unpaid office boy! Previously I had looked forward to the time when I had finished delivering all my lectures as a period when I could relax on board. However, I dealt with this outrageous request as tactfully as I could. Since I had, indeed, finished giving all my lectures for the cruise, I decided to leave the ship in Civitavecchia and fly back from Rome at my own expense. To explain my departure to the Tours Manager I said I had a medical appointment at home. Later, I received a message from P & O's office expressing condolences that I had been "taken ill" at sea and thanking me for my many years of loyal service! It went on to explain that younger lecturers were now required for P & O's new clientele! I kept my feelings to myself, especially since I was still in demand on Cunard ships! After some more years I received a similarly patronising message from Cunard: they had decided that the girls in the Tours office could give "tour talks" to sell their tours. By then I was happily getting more than enough offers to lecture aboard the delightful Yachts of Seabourn!

In those days, crew quarters were not strictly off limits for entertainers in the way in which they are nowadays -

paradoxically so, since now one sometimes finds oneself accommodated through a door marked 'Crew only!' A far cry from the First Class days! But the new Seabourn and Silversea ships are amazingly spacious, being nearly half as large again as the old *Canberra*, with about one third of her total number of passengers!

One occasion when we all trooped down into the Crew Accommodation in the old P & O liners was their Crew Party night. Entertainers would put on a special show for them down below, and I remember a certain lady singer (NOT Vicky!) getting very drunk and disgracefully lewd. Then some of the boys themselves might also perform. There were great sing-songs too. *Himalaya* had her own song, and it was quite something to hear it lustily sung down in the 'Pig and Whistle' as the crew bar was usually called. In those days of all-male stewards and crew, drag was quite popular below decks. There were also stories of gay 'marriages' between crew members, back in those pre-Gay Lib days.

P & O had an arrangement with the Portuguese colony of Goa in India to supply the company with staff. Some of the young boys who joined the ship were eagerly pursued for their favours by the old 'queens' amongst the stewards. I remember one particularly outrageous 'queen,' known as the 'Black Widow.' Presumably because 'she' had a nasty way with her young prey! The Black Widow was a First Class Dining Room Senior Steward in the old *Oriana* – the fastest ship in the fleet in those days, before oil price hikes forced speeds to be moderated in the interests of economy. She could easily reach 30 knots, whereas most cruise ships these days potter around at half that speed. And I heard the Black Widow herself could move pretty swiftly in pursuit of her prey! Another notable 'queen' was the Head Waiter or Steward who used to glide around Canberra's First Class Dining Room, called, I think, the Pacific Restaurant. He was the image, in looks and manner, of the late Kenneth Williams. Indeed, my mother was quite convinced it was he and she questioned him closely about his quiz performances!

The ships' lifts were still operated by smart 'bell boys' with their white gloves tucked under one shoulder epaulette, and (in Cunard ships) their pillbox caps worn at a rakish angle. Naturally, the boys proved a great attraction to any young girls travelling with their parents. One could be left pressing the lift button in vain for many minutes. Eventually the lift would arrive and out would skip some blushing young lady, while the dishevelled lift boy adjusted his pillbox and any other parts of his uniform that needed to be adjusted!

*Bell boys' hand Inspection*

# *14*

# A Princess, a Queen and the Black Watch

*P & O's **Sea Princess,** later **Victoria,** at Santorini*

Once cruising began to take off in the late 1970s, P & O wanted to expand their fleet again. They purchased *Kungsholm,* which had been built for the former Swedish America Line's transatlantic run from Gothenburg to New York. She was converted to increase her capacity to 750 passengers and, from 1981 until 2002, regularly cruised out of Southampton, in tandem with *Canberra* and then with the new *Oriana.* In 1995 she was renamed *Victoria,* to allow the then new addition to the Princess Cruises fleet to be named *Sea Princess.* She was very much the same size as *Chusan* and had the same happy ambience, so she quickly became my favourite ship. She was also the favourite of two of my friends who were retired Anglican clergymen. When we found we were on the same cruise we naturally asked if we could have a table together in the Restaurant. The Head Waiter wasn't happy about this, since - as usual - he was faced with a preponderance of single women who were not happy to dine solely with their sisters. I had to point to him that, if he tried to foist two of these single ladies on my two clerical friends, both confirmed bachelors in their seventies, they would have one hell of a time! He saw my point and we were left undisturbed on our clerical table!

*Victoria*'s Captain was a very friendly, relatively young New Zealander, with whom I had excellent relations. He confided in me that our very efficient female Cruise Director was a former Miss New Zealand. He loved to tease her, which she took mostly in good part. I do recall one occasion, however, when he tried her patience too far. Before heightened Bridge security made it difficult, I was often invited up to the Bridge to give a commentary when we were approaching or leaving port. Early one morning I was in full spate when a very agitated Cruise Director appeared on the Bridge. "Do you know you've woken up the whole ship?" she expostulated. Our naughty Captain had switched my commentary through to all public rooms and cabins! She was NOT amused!

The first cabin to which I was allocated was on A Deck, which pleased me after my demotion to G deck in *Canberra*. It was in a new section of the ship which had been added by P & O when they took over the ship. That night all was revealed: it was directly underneath the dance floor! There seemed to be a great deal of stamping going on above! Were they all dancing a sexy tango, or perhaps the Pasa Doble? I learnt to live with it, having already learnt that most cabins one was allocated as a lecturer would have something wrong! Next year, I was relieved to be moved to a nice outside cabin on D deck, but I discovered it was just inside a large dent in the side of the ship, that had been caused by a collision!

The cinema-cum-theatre in *Victoria* was a lovely room, with panelled wood round the walls. At the sides and back of the auditorium there were modern bronze statues of representatives of the three Estates of the Realm: Clergy, Nobility and Labourers. As a clergyman, I used to enjoy standing in front of the statue of the portly priest!

Before *Victoria* was sold there was a strange chapter in her varied history. 1999/2000 was the centenary of the Union Castle line, whose elegant lavender-painted ships had once plied the route from Southampton to the Cape. I recall many tales of the luxury of the last Union Castle liner *Windsor Castle* and of the rather more down-market, but immensely popular *Reina del Mar,* a one class chartered vessel that specialised in economy cruises. But there was a little difficulty when a group of enthusiasts wanted to arrange a voyage to commemorate the line's centenary: no more Union Castle ships! Nothing daunted, it was arranged to charter *Victoria* and her funnel (but not her hull!) was specially repainted in Union Castle livery!

When it came to *Victoria*'s farewell voyage in Autumn 2002, I was disappointed not to have been selected as her last Port Lecturer, since I had been a frequent lecturer aboard over the 20 years since P & O had converted her. I had just retired from my school chaplain's post, so I was free to undertake cruises during term-time. But the gig went to a fellow lecturer with closer connections. As compensation, I accepted a lectureship aboard Fred Olsen's *Black Watch.* She was (and still is!) another lovely ship, with a distinguished pedigree. Originally built for the former Royal Viking Line as the *Royal Viking Star* in 1971 she was one of the most luxurious cruise ships of her time. But it was difficult for smaller lines to make such ships pay, as both the initially independent Seabourn and Silversea companies were to find later on. Fred Olsen bought the former *Royal Viking Star* in 1996, and gave her one of their line's traditional names, *Black Watch,* after the famous Scottish regiment.

My *Black Watch* cruise in November 2002 proved to be most enjoyable, in spite of my disappointment at missing *Victoria's* final trip. As we sailed at a stately pace from Southampton docks, I noticed a familiar white stern ahead. It was *Victoria* making her final trip down Southampton Water. It almost made up for not being aboard her myself!

*Black Watch* was no longer a luxury cruise ship. One of the extraordinary things that Fred does is to cut his ships in half, insert an extra middle section, and put them together again. I have spent a lot of time walking around the interior of both *Black Watch* and *Boudicaa*, her sister ship, trying to find the joins, so far without success! And a year or so ago Silversea used the same process to extend its *Silver Spirit!* I'll try to check her out when I sail in her next!

I was delighted to find Sir Bernard Ingham, Margaret Thatcher's former Press Secretary, was a fellow lecturer with me aboard the *Black Watch.* His lectures were packed out, with such riveting titles as, 'Travels with the Lioness!' In a quiet moment, I asked him why a man of his age and experience was still doing this sort of thing. "It's the adrenalin, old boy," was his honest answer. And I suppose that's true of most of us lecturers.

Our lecturers' cabins in the *Black Watch* were fairly standard outside passenger cabins on the Main Deck - nothing special, but perfectly adequate. However, the ship's pool was just above us and there was an unfortunate occasion, during a rough passage, when the waters slopped out of the pool and came down to flood Sir Bernard's cabin. By a lucky chance my cabin was on the opposite side of the ship and I escaped the deluge. Now I know why ship's pools are usually emptied when rough weather is anticipated! P & O's new *Oriana* had the longest pool I have encountered in any ship, but it didn't last long! Next time I sailed in her I discovered that the lovely long pool now had a barrier across it, cutting it into two halves. I was told it had been too unstable to leave as one pool. I imagined great rollers breaking over the promenade deck in inclement weather.

*Cunard's **Caronia**, later **Saga Ruby***

# 15

## Cunard Days: *Caronia*

I first spotted Cunard's smart *Caronia* alongside us in, I think, Gibraltar in about 2000. I remember asking a comedian who was working on board *Oriana* with me if he had any knowledge of her and what she was like to work on as a lecturer. "Well," he replied, "I certainly have no complaints. There was a bottle of champagne awaiting my arrival in my passenger cabin." After life "below decks" in *Oriana* this was music to my ears and I determined to get a gig aboard her at the next opportunity. Faced with running just the ageing and uneconomic *QE2,* Cunard were trying to expand into the cruise market and they had chosen to revive the name of their famous luxury liner and cruise ship *Caronia.* Her nickname had been the *Green Goddess*, after the eau-de-nil paintwork of her hull, as well as the Liverpool trams of the same hue. She had been sold, back in 1969.

The new *Caronia* had previously been operated by Cunard as the *Vistafjord,* and was painted white. As *Caronia,* she was given a smart black hull with Cunard's iconic red funnel up above. She had been built as a one class ship, so there was just one elegant restaurant and a large lounge for shows. She also had a cinema, which became my base for lecturing. In rough weather one could usefully wedge the podium between two rows of seats, with room to stand behind it with a bucket behind one in case of an attack of *mal de mer*! Fortunately I never had to use the bucket. I did, however, visit the Doctor's surgery as a precaution and found two sets of pills laid out for our delectation. "What's the difference?" I enquired of the nurse "Well, there's Passenger Pills and Crew Pills," I was informed. "And what is the difference between them?" I asked. "Well, the Passenger pills put the buggers to sleep," I was informed. So I stuck to the Crew Pills!

*Caronia*'s Cruise Director was a lively and charming New Zealander, who had worked hard at building up the ship's reputation as a luxury cruise ship. He had been a show dancer in younger days and, while he must have been approaching sixty as a grandfather, he was still extremely nimble on his feet. He had a whole show of his own with a marvelous Fred Astaire-type virtuoso performance in top hat and tails. When Cunard decided to sell *Caronia,* the Cruise Director was heartbroken. "We've slogged for five years to build her up as a premier cruise ship," he said to me despairingly, "and now they just turn round and tell us it's finished." The truth was, of course, that the new owners of Cunard, the Carnival Corporation of America, had no room for sentiment and in their eyes *Caronia* was just too small to make enough money for their shareholders. It was a pointer towards the future of cruising: bigger and bigger ships, less and less personal care, more and more crowds making movement ashore in some of the most beautiful and precious ports, like Dubrovnik and Venice, almost impossible at peak periods. And the world total of cruise ships is predicted to reach 500! It will be interesting to see if the current Covid-19 virus panic makes any difference to that. I fear it will be the older, smaller vessels that will be most vulnerable.

Although relatively young in her new guise, *Caronia* had already attracted one permanent resident. She was the spitting image of Nancy Reagan, the late US President's wife. She would always sit in the front row of seats for the nightly shows in the Ballroom. At the end of each performance she would be on her feet leading the applause.

# 16

# Cunard Days: *QE2*

During my years of lecturing aboard *Canberra* I had met several passengers who had told me I was missing something by not trying *QE2*. So, when Carnival Corporation decided to drop *Caronia,* and I got the offer to move on to *QE2,* I seized the opportunity.

*QE2* was a very special ship: the 'Greyhound of the Atlantic" She was built to cross the pond in just four and a half days and was still doing that each year in the early Summer and Autumn. It was commonly said that she could sail in reverse faster than most new cruise ships could move forward. There were also summer and autumn cruises and the World cruise at the beginning of each year. Sailing in *QE2,* Lisbon was just a day and a half's sail away from Southampton: just as it had been in P & O's *Oriana* and *Canberra,* before the oil crisis and their consequent slowing down for fuel economy.

*QE2* had had a turbulent history. When construction had started on her, back in John Brown's yard on the Clyde in 1965 she was hailed as the Pride of the Nation. She was the fastest ship ever built in Britain, with a cruising speed of twenty-eight and a half knots. It took her about forty-five miles to stop as well! With her advanced design, she was seen as the 'Miracle ship,' to save both the shipyard and the ailing Cunard company. But others saw her as a 'folly,' destined to fail in the jet age. Construction had dragged on for four and a half years. There were eighteen unions represented amongst the workforce and almost all of them went on strike in turn during the first year of construction. Her launch, by Her Majesty the Queen, had to be put back three times. And then it was found she wasn't really ready!

There were reports of floods in cabins because of defective plumbing. There had been petty theft on a huge scale. There was even a huge hole in the centre of the carpet destined for the ship's main lounge, left by a workman who had cut out enough for his own front room at home!

But, eventually, the new ship settled down and she restored Cunard's fortunes for many years. However, mechanical failures dogged her, even after a refit in 1972, when two rows of balcony cabins were also added on the top deck. These were a foretaste of what is now universal in cruise ships - everyone wants a balcony! The two new Saga ships, *Spirit of Adventure* and *Spirit of Discovery*, for example, promise that every cabin has its own balcony. Yet I remember Commodore Warwick (who had captained *QE2,* following in his father's footsteps) wondering why Cunard's new *Queen Mary 2* needed so many cabins with balconies for the North Atlantic! The truth is that both *QE2* and *QM2* were designed with sweeping open decks and outward facing lounges with cruising in mind during the winter months, when the chill Atlantic is uninviting.

Another innovation in *QE2,* after her first refit, was the addition of a whole shopping mall, including the liner's own Harrods! This also pointed the way to the future, when the on-board spend is now an important contribution to the ship's income. Other refits followed. The old Tourist Class restaurant became the Caronia Restaurant, for the intermediate class between the various Grill classes and the Tourist class, which had its own Mauretania Restaurant. In that restaurant diners had to choose between an early sitting for dinner at 6.45pm and a later one at 8.30pm, whereas one could choose one's time in the more exclusive restaurants.

The various changes in class divisions in the ship meant that travelling in some lifts could be quite an adventure. One would be whisked past certain decks because the lifts had been designed to serve the classes separately, when divisions were more rigid. By the time of my first gig the whole ship was open to all passengers, with the exception of the various Grills and a special upper deck area reserved for Grill passengers. This pattern still continues in *Queen Mary 2* and both *Queen Victoria* and *Queen Elizabeth*, to the amazement of many transatlantic guests.

Midships in *QE2* was a circular Embarkation Hall, very 1960s in décor and nearly always deserted during the voyage. However, I recall finding it packed with Japanese people on one occasion. I burst into laughter. It really was the most bizarre sight! Why they were assembled there and where they were going I never found out! There was also an extensive Library on board, with a proper, rather formidable Librarian in charge.

Aboard the *QE2* I well remember, towards the end, one of the white gloved old queens serving afternoon tea in the Ballroom going around asking all and sundry loudly, "Would you like a tart? We've got plenty of old tarts here!" Such was the level to which the famed 'White Star Service' of the Cunard Line had descended! I'm afraid towards the end of the old days, on both P & O and Cunard, standards of politeness amongst the longstanding staff deteriorated noticeably. The trouble was the unions. If you remember that John Prescott, formerly Deputy Premier in Tony Blair's Socialist Government, had been a Cunard steward and left-wing union activist, back in the Sixties, you will perhaps get the picture. He was not a politician known for his polite manners! I remember once he actually biffed someone who had been heckling him in the street! He has calmed down in recent years and I believe was even invited back by Cunard as a Lecturer aboard *Queen Mary 2*! How times change! Prescott's time in the Merchant Navy included a cruise in

*QE2* from England to New Zealand in 1957, when the former Prime Minister Sir Anthony Eden was recuperating aboard after his resignation following the Suez debacle. Prescott described Eden as a "real Gentleman" and, as well as serving him, was presented by him with the crew boxing trophy, which Prescott had won below decks! Perhaps that all came into his lecture aboard *Queen Mary 2*!

On another occasion, I was queuing up patiently, as one did in the old days, to shake the *QE2* Captain's hand before his 'Welcome Aboard' party. Holding the doors open were a pair of young stewards blatantly and loudly making sarcastic remarks about the passengers, dressed up in their finery, as they filed through! Crew like them knew they had union protection, thanks to the likes of Prescott. Eventually, Cunard had to pay them off at some expense. Sadly, the corollary was that most stewards hired since those days are foreign nationals with no union rights and short contracts.

After I joined *QE2* I was sorry to find that the pleasant custom of being invited to one of the Captain's private cocktail parties in his spacious accommodation up on the Bridge Deck seemed to have fallen into disuse, at least as far as the Port Lecturer was concerned. However a nice surprise came on one of my last cruises aboard: an invitation to join the Captain for drinks in his suite, as in days of yore. "About time too," I had snorted, when I opened the invitation for myself and my companion. Imagine my deflation when we were introduced to the Captain at the party and he thanked my schoolmaster companion, Jon for teaching his son at the King's School, Ely! So much for 'my' invitation as Port Lecturer! Having got over that, I was interested to hear the Captain say that for his next contract he would be in command of P & O's *Oceania* - a lumbering great tub acquired from the Princess Cruise division of Carnival. So not only did *QE2* no longer have a regular Captain, or

Commodore, as in past years, but Captains now moved between the various Carnival brands. Of course this meant there were more opportunities and a better career structure for officers, but I was sad that another tradition had gone. One can hardly expect the same loyalty to a particular ship, or even company, when Captains come and go between them.

*QE2* was a byword for luxury in her heyday. One fifth of the world's supply of caviar, amounting to one ton in weight, was consumed each year, as well as prodigious quantities of champagne. As a guest lecturer, I was invited to three Welcome Aboard and three Farewell parties, one each for Grill, Caronia and Mauretania Class passengers in turn. At the Grill class parties there were enormous tins of caviar displayed in huge wine coolers, surrounded by ice. It was, of course, less lavish at the other two parties, being ready spread on biscuits, but it was still the real McCoy!

Regular guests knew that they could order whatever they fancied to eat in the ship's Restaurants, subject only to giving the chef sufficient notice to prepare it. This could include caviar and lobster every night should they so wish! I recall an occasion when I had a table with the royal florist, who had requested his favourite Sole Veronique, and invited us to share it. It duly arrived for us all, but it *would* be that night that my favourite Dover Sole appeared on the regular menu! I just couldn't face two substantial fish courses!

On the last night of the voyage would come the traditional Baked Alaska Parade. A lump of ice cream encased in meringue, doused in brandy and set fire to! It would then be paraded around the restaurants with sparklers stuck into it. This became an increasingly tacky occasion, with passengers jockeying for position with their cameras and other unseemly behaviour. Stewards also posed for photographs with their tables. It was all a far cry from my early days with P & O when the stewards remained dignified in the background. There were no name tags or fancy uniforms back then! But I suppose it's just part of the Americanisation of British life! With the change of ownership, the currency on board became the mighty dollar, to the dismay of many British passengers, who remembered that *our* taxes had helped to build the heavily subsidized ship in the early days!

The lavish food and wine on board may have had some connection with the fact that I experienced my first attack of gout in *QE2*! We were docked in Lisbon, so I hobbled off into the city to find a chemist. Having explained the problem, I was relieved when the chemist that I had found by the main Santa Apolonia railway station produced some pills he assured me were for gout. I couldn't wait to take one when I got back to the ship! But the pain increased dramatically and so I had to visit and pay the ship's doctor. He was a jolly chap of the old school who explained that the pills I had been given ashore were indeed for treating gout. But the problem was that you couldn't start on them during an attack! Fortunately he had the right pills aboard to deal with an attack. I suppose they were frequently in demand in view of the rich food and drink on board! Passengers who knew I was also a clergyman found it very amusing as I hobbled along! "Over indulging, have we been, vicar?" went the amiable digs....

Another uncomfortable experience of a different kind aboard *QE2* concerned the Lost Teddy Bear Man! It was a perk of lecturers to be able to volunteer to escort ship's excursions. One signed up on a list with one's tour escorting requests and then waited to see the outcome. I was allocated to a guided 'Panoramic' tour, which was really just a ride along the coast to look at some scenic spots. Not very thrilling, but also undemanding to accompany. But I was wrong! One of the participants was a rather strange middle-aged man clutching a large teddy bear. Nothing had been said in my briefing about keeping an eye on this character. After we had made a stop to get out of the coach to admire the view a short walk away I foolishly accepted the Guide's word that everyone was back in the bus. However, on counting heads as we drove on I realized we were one short! Fortunately we hadn't gone far, since we were just driving to find a place where the driver could turn the coach for our return. As we returned to the viewpoint the missing man was still there, frantically waving, with his Teddy Bear. What a relief! I thought little more of it until I was summoned by the Excursion Manager after our return to the ship. "You left a passenger behind!" she rasped at me. "Well, only for five minutes," I replied, explaining the circumstances. It was no good. "He missed part of the tour and I've had to give him a full refund," she stormed. "Well, he only missed turning the bus round," I protested. "I can't possibly offer you any more tour escorting after this," was her reply. To tell the truth that was something of a relief! A 'free' tour always sounds a good idea, but everything has its price! If a party member falls ill, or just falls over, one has to accompany them to the hospital or clinic ashore.

On another occasion, a lady boarding an antique train for a ride, to which I was particularly looking forward, managed to graze her shin on the steep steps. She didn't seem too worried and one of the bandages with which I had been provided had staunched the flow of blood. But that wasn't good enough for her companions! "You must go to hospital," they insisted loudly, so off I had to go for the rest of the day! And when it came to paying the hospital she expected me to fork out! So now I'm very wary about accepting Shore Excursion Managers' offers of tours. And I *never* rely on the guide's counting heads! I think many of the resident ship's staff who used to volunteer if they had time off duty have now decided it isn't worth the hassle. They would rather have some time to themselves.

The new owners of Cunard, the Carnival Corporation of America, had a very hard-nosed approach to their new acquisitions. They had already scandalized many of the loyal, long-serving crew of *QE2* by informing them that, as far as they were concerned, *QE2* was 'just another cruise ship!' They intended to sail at the fullest possible capacity, by discounting fares until the ship was filled. So much for all their publicity about her being a liner, rather than a mere cruise ship! And so much for her former elegant ambience! And yet lecturers were still carefully instructed to refer not to 'cruises' but to 'voyages!' Oh, the hypocrisy of modern marketing! And that was true not only aboard *QE2* and *Queen Mary 2*, which were indeed true liners, but also of the new *Queen Victoria* and *Queen Elizabeth*, which are definitely NOT, being merely standard Carnival Vista class ships, with a cruising speed of around 17 knots. They are the same class of ships as those that sail under the Holland America brand, but with a Cunard style décor added. When Cunard had the bright publicity–driven idea of sailing the then new *Queen Victoria* in tandem with *Queen Mary 2* on a transatlantic crossing the Captain of the *Queen Victoria* remarked to me afterwards on his vessel's lumbering, rolling progress across the ocean, compared to that of the old 'Greyhound of the Seas,' and her successor *Queen Mary 2,* designed deliberately with a low centre of gravity and *four* stabilisers. I had a good example of *Queen Mary 2's* great stability as we sliced through a choppy Bay of Biscay, smoothly overtaking Fred Olsen's little *Braemar,* as she bobbed up and down behind us!

There used to be a very camp Social Host aboard *QE2,* who was well known for his devotion to the ship. He did a wonderful tour of the ship and its impressive collection of memorabilia for novice passengers. I joined it at least twice for sheer enjoyment! And he was unsparing and delightfully indiscreet in his criticism of the new owners and management. I feared for his future employment, but was surprised and relieved to encounter him still working, but now aboard *Queen Mary 2,* when I was lecturing aboard her a year or two later.

At the top of the forward main stairs in *QE2* that led to the Grill cabins and the cinema balcony, between the Upper and Quarter decks, were a pair of lovely portraits by Sir Oswald Birley of King George VI and Queen Elizabeth. They had come from the former Cunard flagship *RMS Queen Elizabeth.* When that liner was retired from service in 1968 the pictures were placed by Cunard Line on permanent loan to Southampton City Council, where the portrait of the Queen Mother graced the Mayor's Parlour for many years.

In 1994 the painting was reclaimed by Cunard Line and placed on display on board the *QE2,* in company with the portrait of King George VI. In 2008, when *QE2* was retired from service and sold to be a floating hotel in Dubai, the royal portraits went with her. They still remain on board, with all the other memorabilia. In 2010 a replica of this painting was created and is now displayed on board Cunard Line's new *Queen Elizabeth* (2010) in the Queens Room.

My happiest, and also saddest, voyage in *QE2* was her final transatlantic cruise in 2008. Most autumns, after the crossing from Southampton to New York, she would sail North to Boston, calling at the exclusive little ports of Bar Harbour and Newport, Rhode Island, with its fabulous millionaire's mansions, and on to Halifax, Nova Scotia, birthplace of Cunard's Founder Sir Samuel Cunard. Then it was up the great St Lawrence River to dock overnight in Quebec, before the return voyage via St John's Newfoundland and back to Southampton for her final crossing.

By 2008 I had already been retired from my Chaplaincy for six years, but I had kept in touch with two boys who were friends and had already come down from Cambridge University. They had some free time before starting their Law Conversion courses, so I asked them if they would like to accompany me and an old school friend of mine B, who was lecturing on films. They jumped at the chance to sail free in such an iconic ship and we had a wonderful three weeks, after I had bribed the Head Waiter in the Caronia Restaurant to give us a nice table together!

Our arrival in New York was as special as I expected. We all got up early and put on our dressing gowns to venture out on deck. Soon we were passing the surprisingly diminutive Statue of Liberty and Manhattan on the Starboard side. And one heard the moving tones of Gershwin's *Rhapsody in Blue* coming over the Tannoy as we passed Ellis Island. It was a very emotional moment. I thought of all those millions of emigrants arriving for a better life in the New World over the years.

After we had docked and braved the grim US Customs officers I particularly enjoyed being guided around New York by my former pupil Josh, whose mother was American and who knew his way around that great city and its metro like a native! I remember being disappointed by Broadway: the 'Great White Way.' It seemed to me disappointingly small and far from white! However, the Empire State Building, shabby as it was by then, and the Chrysler Building lived up to their reputations and I enjoyed the wonderful views of the city.

On the long sea days aboard the ship Josh, Curtis, B and I used to while away the time playing scrabble. Josh was a wizard at this, when he wasn't in the pool or the gym with Curtis. In the evenings, after the glamorous shows, we would all look forward to joining some of the performers at the Midnight Buffet.

And so it ended, with *QE2* sailing down to Dubai a couple of weeks later for conversion into a floating hotel. There was even a plan to install a luxury suite inside her funnel! But still she waits….

*'HM Queen Elizabeth the Queen Consort' by Sir Oswald Birley, hanging on **QE2**'s Forward Main Staircase*

# 17

# Cunard Days: *Queen Mary 2*

I first sailed in Cunard's magnificent new flagship *Queen Mary 2* in October 2004. She had been named by Her Majesty the Queen in January of that year, having been built, to British designs, for the Carnival Corporation of America in the Chantiers de l'Atlantique shipyard in Saint Nazaire, France. The story goes that Her Majesty was not best pleased at finding herself *naming,* rather than launching, an *American* ship, unlike the *QE2* which started life as a British designed, built and operated ship. But at least she sails under the Red Ensign, or the Blue Ensign when an officer in the Royal Naval Reserve is in command. The new ship had already been launched 10 months previously, of course, at St Nazaire. So Her Majesty was described as the ship's "godmother,' an American term for 'celebrities' who perform naming ceremonies, no doubt for a fee! I expect the Queen was also still missing the royal yacht *Britannia,* retired in 1997 and now moored, up in Leith, the port for Edinburgh.

Commodore Ronald Warwick, the last Master of the *QE2,* following his father before him, was also in attendance at the naming ceremony, having previously presided at the laying of *Queen Mary 2's* keel. He had placed two coins, one French, one British, inside for luck, in accordance with naval tradition. Unfortunately, luck failed during a family open day in the St Nazaire shipyard in November, when some wooden scaffolding collapsed and fifteen people died. Another unlucky incident came a couple of years later, with the loss of one of her propulsion pods, after scraping the side of the shipping channel at Fort Lauderdale in Florida. Commodore Warwick, who had been persuaded to postpone his retirement to command the new ship, was swiftly retired, although he later appeared on board *Queen Victoria* in charge of a kind of souvenir shop! Fortunately, since *Queen Mary 2* had been given four engine pods, rather than the two with which lesser vessels had to make do, her speed was not drastically affected. Nonetheless, she was forced to cut some of her calls in the West Indies and I read that disgruntled passengers tried to stage a revolt! Carnival Corporation subsequently sued Rolls-Royce, the suppliers of the pods, in the US for 100 million dollars. They were awarded 24 million dollars by the court.

*Queen Mary 2* was, and remains, the largest true liner ever built. I was extremely impressed by her elegant décor and particularly by the magnificent auditorium in which I was to lecture, which also doubled as a planetarium. Sadly, there was no *Caronia* class Restaurant, so it was a choice between the Grills and the huge, two-sitting Mauretania Restaurant. Needless to say, I was allocated to the latter! This was a very impressive room, with a grand flight of stairs down from its entrance. There seemed, however, to be a shortage of the elegant dining chairs that had been specially designed and made for the ship. It emerged that they had not been able to cope with the girth and weight of some of the American guests, so sturdier versions had to be ordered!

True to Cunard tradition, *Queen Mary 2* has a large elegant ballroom, known as the Queen's Room, as in *QE2*. But this one is rather unusually situated, down on Deck 3 in the aft section of the ship- not the best position for unsteady dancing feet! Or for waiters struggling to serve tea elegantly in their white gloved hands! But the ship's extraordinary stability overcomes most of the motion of the ocean. Access to the Queen's Room is by corridors lined with excruciatingly vulgar pictures, which were offered for sale by auction, up in the Winter Garden, and often sold at absurd prices! But the

Room itself is presided over by fine bust of the young Queen Mary, consort to King George V.

On my first gig aboard her we cruised the Western Mediterranean, calling at Livorno amongst other ports, so guests could visit Pisa and Florence in particular. Unfortunately the heavens opened and a party of Japanese was considerably delayed on their return from Florence. We had to wait for them as night fell, since they were on an official tour. This meant it was already dark and, with a strong wind blowing, the Harbour Master felt he couldn't take the risk of allowing the ship to sail. There had already been one wreck just out of Livorno a year or so before!

This delay meant that the remainder of our itinerary had to be adjusted and it was decided to abort the next call at Gibraltar. That raised a problem for me, as I was expecting to be joined there by an old friend who would sail back to England with me. My brother in Spain, attempted to contact my friend Andy to put him off, but with no success, since Andy was already on his way from Malaga to Gibraltar. Then I was told that the ship's Agent had to come out by boat from Gibraltar in order to rendezvous with us to sign duty-free papers. Gibraltar, of course, had Duty Free Status. It would therefore be possible for my friend to come out with the Agent to join the ship at sea. This entailed his having to climb up the ship's huge black side with his bag strapped go his back! Fortunately Andy made it and lived to make many more recordings of the BBC's long-running serial 'The Archers,' in which he plays the role of Adam. I only wish I had a film of his ascent!

A later voyage in *Queen Mary 2* had its own very different excitements. I was to fly down to the Gulf to join her in Dubai, on the last leg of her world cruise. I flew down with B, my film lecturer friend, and his friend Curtis, a former pupil of mine, on a very comfortable Emirates flight. I had heard of the exotic delights of Dubai with its high-rise and high-end hotels and wonderful airport, but I found it resembled rather a very dusty building site! True, there were many palm trees inside the airport building, but they were so dusty it wasn't clear if they were real trees or fakes!

When we reached the ship we were faced with an enormous queue to board. This is one of the unavoidable annoyances of mega-ships: however efficient they are aboard in checking guests on and off through two entrances, they are in the hands of the Port Authority for the arrangements ashore. Fortunately, after the Captain had seen me in the queue and greeted me profusely, we were whisked aboard! Later, faced with a similar queue in pouring rain to board in Vigo, my friend was able to go straight on because a lady on the tour he had been escorting had fallen over on the dockside. He was lucky it hadn't happened earlier, when he would have had to take her to hospital ashore!

From Dubai we sailed past Oman, Yemen and the Horn of Africa, with its lurking pirates. Fortunately, none of them seemed keen to take on our mighty liner! Then we steamed up the Red Sea towards the Suez Canal with a call at Sharm el Sheik on the Sinai Peninsula. This rather tacky resort used to be visited by the likes of Tony Blair for some winter sun to top up their perma-tans, until terrorism took hold there. But I could find nothing of interest ashore.

Our next call at Safaga on the Red Sea, was very different. I was to accompany the ship's tour to Luxor: all 150 miles or so across the desert! Each coach was provided with two armed escorts, one in front and one at the back! I found this more alarming than reassuring, but the journey passed without incident. Luxor was more than worth the journey. It's on the eastern bank of the Nile and was the site of ancient

Thebes, the pharaohs' capital at the height of their power, during the 16th to the 11th centuries B.C. After a drive through the pleasant modern resort, it was off to the first of the 2 huge, surviving ancient monuments: the graceful Luxor Temple, with its impressive statues of ancient Pharaohs. After that, we progressed to the Karnak Temple, a mile north, which is much more a complex of impressive ruins than one complete building. Then it was time for lunch at the Winter Palace Hotel, which goes back to Victorian days, although the security x-ray procedure at the entrance was more reminiscent of a modern airport!

Next on the agenda were the royal tombs of the Valley of the Kings and the Valley of the Queens, over on the river's west bank. This was for me the highlight of the trip, especially when we visited the tomb of Tutankhamun, discovered in 1922 by Howard Carter, backed by Lord Carnarvon. It was rather tourist-worn by 2007, before a major conservation project the next year, but it was still immensely atmospheric. I remembered the famous curse of the Pharaohs and hoped it was no longer in operation! The complex has a total of 63 tombs, but mercifully we only went into a couple! The tombs date from the 16th to 11th century BC and are decorated with fascinating scenes from Egyptian mythology.

After passing Ismailia, with its large mosque and minaret, it wasn't long before we entered the Suez Canal. It was amazing to see, looking down from the great ship, men pumping water to irrigate their crops, just as they would have done 2000 or more years ago. Although NOT by the side of this canal, of course! I was invited to give a commentary as we sailed; but, since the total transit takes more than 12 hours and tends to become monotonous, I was only required to point out places of interest as we passed! The canal is 120 miles long and has no locks, since it is all at sea level. So we joined a small convoy and proceeded at a sedate 8 knots, to reduce erosion of the tall sandy banks.

I couldn't help but remember the Suez crisis, which took place in 1956, when I was still a schoolboy in Hammersmith. Col. Nasser, the Egyptian leader, had nationalised the canal, which had been the property of an Anglo-French company. Britain had gone to war in an attempt to get it back, in collusion with Israel and France. America refused to back us and Britain's subsequent humiliation led to Sir Anthony Eden's resignation as Prime Minister and his recuperation aboard *QE2*!

When we were through the canal, we headed for Port Said, once a byword for squalor and corruption, but now just a rather nondescript, shabby Arab port. The purpose of our call was to visit Cairo and the pyramids. I opted for a city tour, visiting a great mosque with a marvelous clock, rather than a museum visit to see King Tutankhamun. Then followed a short drive to see the famous pyramids, which are now virtually in a Cairo suburb. They still impress, but the place was overrun with touts offering camel rides, photographs, papyrus, 'genuine' Egyptian scarabs and heaven knows what else. Later we joined a Nile cruiser for a short excursion and lunch on board. Having been warned of these boats' fearsome reputation for causing stomach upsets, I determined to be cautious. In the buffet queue I was appalled to watch a guest just in front of me drop a kebab on the floor, pick it up and make to put it back on the buffet table! Fortunately I was able to prevent this mistake!

Our next call was scheduled to be Alexandria, of which I have happy memories, when we docked there in Chandris Cruises' *Fantasia,* back in the Sixties. It was during the Egyptian/Israeli conflict and I spent a very scary night aboard ship, while most of the passengers went off to Cairo overnight. The Egyptian navy were dropping depth charges in the harbour to keep off Israeli divers, who were said to be attempting to sabotage ships in the harbour, by attaching limpet mines to them! So, every time I heard a bang echoing through the ship, I wondered if it was us or them being hit! The next day I went on a fascinating trip along the coast by myself on a public bus, past smart resorts, to visit ex-King Farouk's palace. There one was shown round by a jet black attendant from the Sudan who took great delight in showing us a fine selection of what were claimed to be Farouk's drugs! Later that evening I enjoyed exploring ashore with a retired sailor from my group, who wanted to revisit old haunts. It seemed little had changed, as we were besieged with all kinds of mostly depraved offers, including bottles of whisky, stealthily produced and exhibited, along with dubious postcards and offers of 'companionship!'

When we were due to dock in Alexandria, all those years later in *Queen Mary 2*, we found ourselves to be still at sea! The wind had got up overnight and it was touch and go as to whether we would be able to get alongside the harbour pier. Eventually, about 11am, the Captain announced it was too risky and that we would be sailing on to Piraeus for Athens, where we would have an extra night in port. This was a great disappointment to everyone. I had been extolling the attractions of the city and now my pictures were going to be all that they would see of it - and of Cairo! But these things happen on cruises, much as the companies try to gloss over them! At least in Athens we had a chance to see the wonderful *Son et Lumiere* show below the Acropolis that we would have missed without our extra night there!

HM Queen Mary, Queen's Room, *Queen Mary 2*

# 18

## Some more fellow guests and lecturers

A number of celebrities, particularly from the Entertainment world, used to cruise regularly. The late Jimmy Savile was a frequent passenger in *QE2*. Indeed his photograph was proudly displayed amongst a collection of shipboard memorabilia in a display case at the top of the main forward staircase. He was popular on board since he was always willing to be interviewed and talk (for no fee) and these occasions always commanded full houses. On my last voyage in *QE2* I agreed to help the ship's Catholic Chaplain by acting as a Eucharistic Minister to administer one of the two chalices at the well-attended Sunday Mass. The other Eucharistic Minister was Jimmy Savile! He was a devout Roman Catholic, which made the terrible revelations that came out later about his sexual transgressions particularly hard to forgive.

Des O'Connor, the comedian and chat show host, was another frequent passenger, this time aboard P & O's *Canberra*. He generally preferred to keep himself to himself. The late Frankie Howard was also a regular P & O passenger. I sailed with him in P & O's *Victoria* towards the end of his life. After dinner he used to come up to the Promenade Deck most evenings, to sit with his companion and stare at the sea. He always looked extremely glum, but gamely agreed to put on a special show for the crew, with whom he was a great favourite.

On one early cruise in *Chusan* we learnt that Richard Marsh, a Labour Party politician and Transport Minister, who eventually became Chairman of nationalised British Railways, was sailing with us. Of course, as a good Socialist,

116

he occupied a spacious First Class suite. However, he proved to be a very convivial sort of chap and we 'Entertainers' were duly entertained by him to drinks in his suite on several evenings. In those far-off days food - even in First Class - was not always easily available in the late evenings, and so a group of us raided the ship's Galley for some sandwiches. We were discovered by the Nightwatchman on his rounds, who duly took our names and cabin numbers and informed us we would be reported and be "up before the Old Man (Captain)." When we pointed out this included a Minister of the Crown who was sailing as a First Class passenger we heard no more…

Another notable P & O passenger in those far-off days was the Dowager Marchioness of Reading. One used to pass her seated with her companion in the shade of the Promenade Deck, hard at work on her needlework. It was a scene straight from the days of the British Raj! I read recently that she once wrote to the *Daily Telegraph* to advise that the best way to deal with sex offenders was to castrate them! The paper declined to publish it. On another occasion, in 1998, she wrote to the *Spectator* expressing support for football hooligans. "We are a nation of yobs," wrote the doughty old marchioness, who was already almost 80. "Without that characteristic, how did we colonise the world? Now that we don't have a war, what's wrong with a good punch-up?" Her husband, the first Marquess, had been by turns Lord Chief Justice of England, Viceroy of India, and Foreign Secretary!

It was easy to imagine in the old P & O ships, as one strolled the Verandah deck and observed the games of deck quoits, the elderly ladies on their steamer chairs, the couples briskly doing their 'eight-times-round-the-deck-equals-one-mile' promenade and the stewards going the rounds with a box of ice creams, that one was returning from a spell in British India. Not for nothing was P & O sometimes called the

'Exiles' Line!' This thought used to come to me particularly as we crossed the grey Bay of Biscay on the last day of the voyage.

Amongst my fellow lecturers aboard the Cunard ships was the late Sheridan Morley, theatre critic, author and broadcaster, and son of the actor Robert Morley. I'd been a contemporary of Sheridan's at Oxford, my college, St John's (now a hotbed of feminism!), being next door to his college, Trinity. The late David Frost, who was most famous for his devastating television interview of former President Nixon, sadly died while lecturing aboard *QE2*

There was usually a former Concorde jet pilot aboard as a lecturer and they were mostly extremely pleasant and sociable fellows. This was a 'hangover' from the days when Cunard had the clever marketing ploy of arranging for passengers to fly Concorde supersonically in one direction and to sail the other way in *QE2*. The combined fare was less than a single ticket on Concorde.

After I joined the new *Oriana* as Port Lecturer, I was delighted to discover Dick Francis, the novelist and former jockey, was sailing with us. He was the Queen Mother's favourite novelist, as I was reminded recently when the Prince of Wales broadcast from his study at Birkhall on Royal Deeside, up in Scotland. He was isolating there with the Duchess of Cornwall, as he recovered from the Corona virus. Prince Charles inherited Birkhall from his grandmother, to whom he was very close. There, on the shelves behind him in his study, were some of Dick Francis's novels! I believe Francis used to present them to his distinguished fan, with her great love of horses! And no doubt Camilla enjoys them too! Dick Francis was promoting his latest novel on board with some signing sessions. He was travelling with his son and daughter-in-law, whom I knew through friends at Bloxham School, where his son taught. So I was invited to a nice party in their suite.

Another fellow lecturer with whom I first sailed in *QE2* was John Maxtone-Graham. I shall never forget his enormous sense of style and charismatic stage manner. He had served in the United States Marine Corps during the Korean War and then worked as a Broadway stage manager. He was the author of a best selling book about the great Atlantic liners, *The Only Way to Cross*, published in 1972. He followed this up with a series of books about other great Atlantic liners, including the *Titanic*, the *Normandie, Mauretania, Queen Mary* and the *SS United States*. Thus he had copious resources of material for his very successful lecturing career. Always happy to talk about ships with other ship buffs aboard, he was a very snappy dresser and I recall being impressed by the tartan trews he usually wore with his dinner jacket in the evenings. These emphasized his Scots ancestry, although he was born in America. His delivery was best described as "Transatlantic.'

I recall one occasion when John broke off lecturing in mid-flow. He had noticed a member of the audience recording him. "Please stop that at once," his peremptory tones rang out, "These talks are *my* copyright and not to be recorded!" On another occasion he gave a thorough account of the old style of table service one used to receive in grand hotels like Claridges. "But now," he concluded dolefully, "even *they* serve plated meals." I knew what he meant, since I could still recall proper silver service aboard the old P & O ships, where the table steward (not 'waiter' in those days) would hand round the vegetables in a silver dish so one could help oneself. Nowadays it's all what an old lady I used to know called, "Dog's dinner!" In other words, all ready plated up, so one can't choose the quantity one wants of the various items.

My last sight of John was as a guest aboard one of the new larger Seabourn ships. Although in his eighties, he was as elegant and poised as ever.

A regular speaker I met first in P & O ships, and later in *QE2* and *QM2,* was the former royal florist, Howard Franklin. He spoke with authority about royal matters and gave entertaining accounts of his part in "doing the flowers" for great royal events, like Prince Charles and Princess Diana's wedding. I believe Howard had some connection with P & O's management that enabled him to hang on to his outside passenger cabin, while the rest of us were moved down below decks. He was also often a guest at the Captain's table. He became – and remains - a good friend and we swapped many tales about ships we had known and the various characters on board. Later Howard was able, like myself, to transfer to the delightful Silversea ships, where he continues, at the time of writing, to entertain in his inimitably stylish manner.

Another 'celebrity speaker' aboard Q*ueen Mary 2* was Paul Burrell, the late Princess Diana's butler, who was later about to be charged with theft of her property, until Her Majesty the Queen intervened to halt the case. I believe he lectured on how to lay up tables correctly, amongst other things! This would be irrelevant today in many ships- including, sadly, Cunard, since guests are no longer provided with a 'full cover' on their dining tables. I asked a Head Waiter why, and he replied it was done "for hygienic reasons!" I suspect it is done to spare 'new' cruisers from the embarrassment of not knowing that one works inward from outer implements. And finger bowls for messy dishes are quite unheard of, yet alone Rose Water, as one of the old-style Housemasters at Harrow used to provide at his dinner parties! (Though not at House Lunch! One could envisage only too clearly what would have ensued had the 'Bloods' of the Philathletic Club encountered such items full of Rose water!)

*Queen Mary 2* alongside in Boston

# 19

# Sailing with Saga

## *Saga Ruby*

When Carnival decided to pull the plug on Cunard's attempt to recreate their former luxury cruise ship *Caronia* the crew were as disappointed as I was. She had been the former white-painted *Vistafjord,* repainted in Cunard's smart black livery. Fortunately, however, Saga cruises, who already operated *Caronia*'s ageing older sister, the former *Sagafjord,* as the *Saga Rose,* were looking for another ship and, after a refit, *Caronia* took on a new lease of life as *Saga Ruby*, this time repainted in dark blue!

Saga had moved into cruising back in 1997, with the purchase of *Sagafjord*, so this was a natural expansion. I had been booked by Saga as the Port Lecturer on the maiden voyage of the *Saga Rose*. Unfortunately, however, there had been a fire on board during the refit, which meant the cruise had to be cancelled. Since I had already prepared all my lectures I was not best pleased. Saga offered no compensation to me as an unpaid Lecturer, but they *had* issued me with a passenger ticket. I was able to take this to the Small Claims Court and Saga were obliged to pay me the cost of that ticket, since it was effectively to have been my pay. Since then I have *never* been issued with a passenger ticket when lecturing! Have I been put on a black list? But, fortunately, I have also had no more cruises cancelled; that is, until Covid-19 struck!

I admit to being somewhat dubious about what Saga might make of *Caronia*, but I was delighted to find her much improved. And I was told by someone in the know that Saga had to organize a massive clean-up of the galley when they took over! One therefore wonders how *Caronia* had previously passed the rigorous port hygiene inspections!

Saga carry several lecturers on each of their cruises, as well as a Port or Destination Lecturer, so I was able to persuade my agent that an old school and college contemporary of mine, who had been Head of Film Studies at a leading school and was also the author of a learned book on cinema, titled, *Next Train's Gone*, would be a valuable additional lecturer. We had already worked together in *QE2*. B duly prepared an interesting series of talks on different kinds of film comedy, illustrated with appropriate clips. But his characteristic sense of mischief led him to include a clip from *The Closet*, a French comedy in which a character rides a float in a gay pride parade, wearing a huge condom on his head! The sedate senior Saga audience, as might have been expected, received this spectacle with some perturbation, the more mobile ones staggering out waving their sticks and muttering imprecations! B decided against any future offers from Saga cruises! Would he *also* have been put on a black list otherwise?

On my second cruise in the *Ruby* I had been shown at Embarkation to a spacious Forward cabin, which had been adapted for wheelchair users. But, no sooner had I unpacked, than I had a message informing me that the cabin was now required for a wheelchair passenger! I had to repack and move. I was then put in a very small claustrophobic cabin. This didn't bode well! I sought out the Cruise Director. "Leave it with me," she said. Later on, she came back with the news that one of Saga's directors was on board and that he was disembarking in Copenhagen, the first port of call, so I could then move into his cabin. This proved to be a magnificent suite up on the top deck, above the Bridge. My joy was slightly modified when we set sail. The newly added cabin vibrated loudly! Definitely not 'Good Vibrations,' like the Beach Boys' song! I was up most of the night wedging pieces of tissue paper into cracks around the edge of the ceiling to stop the noise. When I awoke in the morning, the cabin was decorated with all these pieces of toilet paper that had worked loose during the night. When the Butler arrived with my morning tea his expression was worthy of that old end-of-the–pier bioscope, "What the Butler Saw!'

## Sailing down to Cape Town

January 2009 saw me setting off in the *Ruby* on a real voyage of adventure, all down the African coast to ports that hadn't seen a passenger ship for twenty or thirty years and ending in Cape Town. Knowing that Saga usually carried several lecturers, I had offered talks on the history of the various ports and countries we would be visiting. However, a few days before sailing I was told they hadn't been able to find a Port Lecturer. Could I cover that as well? Not one to refuse a challenge, I agreed, while making it clear that I hadn't visited a number of the African ports. But then neither would anyone else have done! Needless to say, being Saga, an indomitable old lady emerged aboard, who had sailed the same route about 50 years prior! Thankfully, she let me off lightly!

We called first at Funchal, Madeira, next Santa Cruz de Tenerife and then Dakar in Senegal, West Africa. I remembered that it had been quite a frequent port of call in bygone days, but it seemed to have dropped off the cruise schedules. Once ashore, the reasons soon became apparent.

Dakar was once a tiny settlement on the Cape Verde peninsula, but it has just grown and continues to grow: a mixture of the luxurious and the primitive. Its origins were closely linked with the slave trade, first under the Portuguese, then the Dutch and finally the French, who moved the settlement from the off-shore island of Goree, where one can still see the infamous House of Slaves. Surprisingly, this vile trade was dominated by 'signares' - the daughters of white colonists and slave women. It was a largely matriarchal, slave-worked society. Today only the grim 'House of Slaves' and the memorial to the slaves remain to be visited on Goree. But, as Goree declined, Dakar grew. With the coming of the railway (and Dakar Station is a fine example of French Colonial architecture) peanut growing eventually filled the gap left by the abolition of the slave trade. Fishing is now the most important industry, as a visit to the market confirmed, followed by tourism. The ground nuts come third nowadays. Islam is the most powerful faith and the Muslim brotherhoods (a kind of Islamic freemasonry) dominate much of the country's economy.

As soon as we attempted to leave the rather decrepit shuttle bus provided to the town centre we were surrounded by a very vociferous collection of touts and would-be vendors. Today Dakar is one of West Africa's biggest conurbations, with around two and a half million people, many of whom are living in dire poverty. Most guests took one look and remained in the bus to return immediately to the ship! I braved the crowd and managed to shake them off, after walking a block or so towards the coast. But it was useless. As soon as one stopped another person would make a beeline towards one! After taking refuge for a while in one of the French-built luxury hotels above the beach, I had to face the same pestering all the way back to the pick-up place. Mercifully, a bus was waiting!

As we set sail in choppy seas, I was reminded that it was off the coast of Senegal that the *Medusa* was shipwrecked, driven aground on one of the many sandbars of the Arguin bank that lie off the coast in those waters. Once you've seen Gericault's magnificent painting, *The Raft of the Medusa* in the Louvre, you never forget it. But the *Medusa* was captained by an inexperienced French aristocrat, the Vicomte Hugues Duroy de Chaumareys, whereas *we* had a very experienced English captain!

Freetown, Sierra Leone was our next port. Sierra Leoneans joke that when God created the world he endowed the country with such a wealth of natural resources, including diamonds and gold, that the angels protested that it was unfair on other countries. "Don't worry," God replied, "Just look at the people I've put there!" This seemed unfair to the majority of the smiling people who greeted us, but the country's history since independence - a series of military coups, 23 years of one party rule and a civil war lasting 11 years - serves to confirm the wry joke.

Back in the sixteenth century, Sierra Leone was another important slaving centre, like Dakar, but in this case under the British. Sir John Hawkins, knighted by Queen Elizabeth I for his services in the war against Spain, operated a lucrative trade in slaves - he can be seen as the father of the American slave trade. And his cousin, Sir Francis Drake, was also heavily involved in it!

The 'slaving factory' on Bunce Island, 30 miles up river from Freetown, is a horrific relic of the trade. There was a particular link with Charleston, South Carolina to supply the rice planters there with slave labour. After the American Revolution, American merchants were forbidden to buy slaves or any goods arriving in British ships. But the slavers got round this by using Danish ships! A cannon dated 1780 from a Danish ship was pointed out to me on Bunce island to prove it!

The buildings themselves are now heavily shrouded in creeper and tropical vegetation and are in an advanced state of decay. This made them less intimidating, and it was difficult to imagine the horrific scenes they must have witnessed. But it's still possible to see the names slaves left, carved on some of the trees, and the tombstones of slaves who had died there. It was a chastened group that returned to *Saga Ruby*. Fortunately the movie 'Amistad,' which gives a vivid picture of this foul trade at its peak, was not being shown that evening! In any event, President Trump would have dismissed it as "false history!"

During the War of American Independence, Britain promised freedom to over 3000 persons of African descent, if they deserted their American rebel masters and remained loyal to Britain. Those who responded found refuge in New York, and from there many made their way across the Atlantic to London, Liverpool and Bristol As early as 1772 there had been a legal case that established that, once freed, a slave could not be returned to his master. So, in 1787, the first group of 411 people, mostly black but including some 60 white women, arrived in Sierra Leone from Britain to set up 'The Province of Freedom.' This was Freetown's origin, although a third of them were dead within three months with malaria and other diseases. They bought the area from a Temne herdsman called King Tom, but his successor King Jimmy evicted them and burnt the settlement to the ground. A second attempt in 1792 with over 1,200 settlers had more luck, with the support of William Wilberforce, the great anti-slavery campaigner, and others. More settlers arrived from Nova Scotia and, after slavery was abolished, some 70,000 're-captives,' freed from slave ships, followed. After Napoleon's defeat at Waterloo, many of the African soldiers who had served in British regiments were pensioned off to the colony. Hence villages with names like Wellington and Waterloo, which were founded by the former soldiers.

When I told a friend who knows West Africa that we were going to Takoradi, our next port, he wondered why! It's a Ghanaian industrial port and they obviously hadn't seen a passenger liner for a very long time. I was struck by the wonderful smiles with which we were greeted. Of course, white teeth in black faces stand out particularly well, but there was genuine warmth in our reception. Most people seemed to be living in very poor conditions- there were lines of shanties just above the waterfront. Some of the gestures the young men made toward our group were unambiguously sexual, but one put this down to natural joie de vivre!

As it was a Sunday, some of us sought out the large church further back in town. We found a packed congregation in the huge hangar-like building. When the time came for the collection there was no passing of the plate or bag. Oh no! Members of the congregation got up and danced up the aisle to place their offerings on a large plate in front of the altar! I can still see the huge black mamas swaying their way up the aisle in time to the African beat! It was all a great change from the Sunday hymn sandwich on board ship with the Filipino choir! But both of them put the reticence of the average English congregation to shame!

Takoradi also has one of the largest markets in West Africa. It's not for the faint-hearted! A disorientating frenzy of colour, noise and smells. Lorries full of yams are unloaded, machete-wielding coconut sellers lop off tops and stick in straws, and a bewildering array of goods are paraded past you on head-tops: sunglasses, dried fish, flip flops and colanders. Further into the centre, meanwhile, an almost exclusively female sales force hawks colourful vegetables, chilli peppers, fish and a variety of meat. It was certainly a full-on experience!

Lome, capital of Togo, on the Gulf of Guinea, was our next call. A Nigerian pupil of mine had told me it was a sort of pleasure city - West Africa's answer to Las Vegas, perhaps - but all I could find was an excellent choice of mainly French restaurants! However, the people seemed to retain an air of nonchalance unusual in West Africa and they were also very friendly. Lome had been the capital of a German colony and the neo-Gothic cathedral bears witness to that. After the First World War most of it became a French protectorate until full independence came in 1960.

There have been various attempts to modernize the city since then, the main evidence being the city's first skyscraper, the Hotel du Deuxieme Fevrier, a 37 storey marble and glass tower. Back in 2008 it was in the middle of nowhere, having been built as part of a plan to get the Organisation of African Unity's headquarters transferred to Lome. But the plan never came off and the hotel, then one of Africa's most luxurious, remained virtually empty for years. It was looking pretty dusty when we passed it! There's also a vast Palais du Congres and various showy ministry buildings with dusty gold-tinted glass. This was all down to Etienne Eyadema, a former sergeant in the military, who staged the first coup in Africa in 1963. He remained in power for 38 years, only to be replaced by his son! But he was defeated in elections in 2007 and a period of upheaval followed.

The driving was absolutely hair-raising! Our bus was also interesting. Guests often complain about deficient air conditioning on excursion buses, but that was not a problem - this one relied on holes in the floor! There were none of the usual complaints about the microphone not working either, since there was none! The mandatory 'rest room stop' was interesting. We were getting increasingly desperate to find somewhere, so I got the driver to stop at a local school, made a quick recce inside to ascertain where the facilities were located, primitive as they were, got the caretaker's permission and shepherded my flock into the school loos! Naturally, we had all been warned to bring our own toilet paper with us, which was just as well…

Recovering from that, we drove next to a beach establishment a little way out of town for a very acceptable lunch. Then it was time to gird our loins for the huge Fetish Market! It seemed to cater more for tourists than witch doctors when we visited, with notices demanding an admission fee. We were warned not to touch any of the objects on display, as we would then become liable to buy them. The variety of human and animal heads, wizened dried monkeys, skulls, rotting bird carcasses and all kinds of other creatures was truly sick-making, both because of the stench and the revolting sights. I don't think anyone was remotely tempted to touch, to the evident disappointment of the ghoulish stallholders! Voodoo dolls and all the imaginable and unimaginable ingredients of traditional medicine and religion were also in abundance! It's the largest such market in West Africa and people come from all over to consult the voodoo priests, the feticheurs. The majority of the Togolese still practice animist religion, and even the Christian and Muslim minorities incorporate some traditional practices into their beliefs. This, of course, is just the sort of place where the Corona pandemic could have started and one hopes the authorities have closed it down for ever.

*The Voodoo Market in Lome, Togo*

Back on the ship, I wondered whether the ship's doctor and chaplain would find a decline in attendances with all the voodoo paraphernalia available in the market; but, mercifully, Customs prohibit the export of such items!

Next up on our cruise was Limbe, the port of Cameroon. It had been advertised that we would be sailing up the great River Wouri to dock in Douala, Cameroon's economic capital, but I think we were actually much better off staying in Limbe, where we tendered in, with Mount Cameroon directly above us. There was more slave history, of course, but I preferred to concentrate on the impressive scenery here, on a tour through the tea plantations on the slopes of Mount Cameroon and the former German capital of Buea ('Beautiful Buea' aptly named!). The Germans made it their capital because of the cooler climate up on the mountain slopes. The President occupies the former German Governor Von Puttkamer's palace as his summer residence, but we were told he doesn't like anyone taking pictures of it! Bad for his image, I suppose! But definitely not worth being arrested! The University is up here too, and we were amused to see large 'Speak English' signs had been put up. So thoughtful of them…but, it emerged, they were not really intended for our benefit, nor did they seem to have been very effective! But at least they weren't speaking German! After the botanic garden, we went on to the wildlife centre, where there were charming, but smelly chimpanzees and other primates. We tried to think whom they reminded us of! There were also dramatic views of the volcanic landscape left by the eruption of Mount Cameroon in 1999, but the 62 steps up for the best view proved too many for some!

Our next port of call, the lovely former Portuguese island of Sao Tome, set in the Gulf of Guinea together with its neighbouring island of Principe, was for me one of the high points of our cruise. It's the second smallest African country in terms of population, after the Seychelles, and it's the smallest Portuguese-speaking country in the world. The islands are part of an extinct volcanic range and they sit across the Equator. Uninhabited before the Portuguese arrived, they became Africa's foremost exporter of sugar. 3,000 Jewish children were sent from Portugal to work in the plantations. Later, slaves were brought over from the African mainland to bolster the workforce. Brazil eventually undercut the sugar production and now coffee and cocoa have taken pride of place.

We were informed we were the sixth cruise ship *ever* to have called at the island, so we got a big welcome. There were many beautiful old Portuguese colonial style buildings, but most of them were pretty poorly maintained, with the exception of a few old estate houses that have been converted into hotels. The official buildings - the Presidential Palace, the Supreme Court and the Casa de Cultura - are all painted in an attractive pink wash, which reminded me of the

Presidential palace down in Buenos Aires, the Casa Rosada, but on a smaller scale.

My favourite dish in Madeira, the vicious looking espardete fish from the depths of the ocean, served with fried bananas, was widely available in Sao Tome, but I was cautious about local hygiene. Likewise with the palm-wine offered by street vendors! The local currency, called the Dobra, is a restricted one, but American dollars seemed to be widely accepted. The people were charming and friendly, especially the children, who were thrilled with the sweets and pens that some thoughtful guests had brought for them.

Once you get out of town, Sao Tome is covered with a beautiful, thick jungle. We saw amazing black rock formations in the shape of pillars ('picos' in Portuguese) apparently rising out of nowhere, some going up to around 5,000 feet. They are actually columns of magma, left after the volcanoes that surrounded them have been eroded away. In places the jungle seems to go right down to the sea. It reminded me of 'Bali Hai' in 'South Pacific!'

And the beaches! All kinds - black sandy ones, gravel ones and white sandy ones. The one thing they all had in common was a background of jungle and palm trees. They were mainly used by fishermen, with their primitive cut-out boats, made from a single tree trunk, and people having a rest from their work. It's that sort of laid-back place. They love to grab a coconut and chop it into pieces with their machetes, which seem to be commonly carried by many - so no need for alarm!

Crime is extremely low and there are still only about 13,000 tourists a year between the two islands of Sao Tome and Principe. For birdwatchers it's a paradise - the islands boast the highest density of endemic species worldwide, including the world's largest weaver bird, *Ploceus grandis*, a species of bird in the family Ploceidae. It's endemic to São Tomé Island and can climb trees and branches, rather like a treecreeper or sittella. Its natural habitat is subtropical or tropical moist lowland forests.

The largest sunbirds in the world are also found on Sao Tome. They are unmistakeable with their thin, downward-curving bills and brush-tipped tubular tongues, adapted specially for nectivory: they feed on (you've guessed it) nectar. In total, the islands are home to some 28 endemic species, with 17 found on Sao Tome and 11 on Principe. I would dearly love to have been able to explore the other island, Principe, as well, but it's only accessible via a 35minute flight or a longish boat trip and we had to sail at 4pm, so that was out! One place I *did* manage to explore, however, was the 'laboratory' of the famous chocolatier Claudio Corallo. His 100% cacao chocolate bars are a chocoholic's dream come true!

From Sao Tome it was a three days' sail down to Walvis Bay, in Namibia. It's very much of a staging post on the voyage down to Cape Town and offers little in the way of attractions of its own. However, there are two very interesting excursion possibilities: the very Germanic old town of Swakopmund down the coast or an expedition in the Namibian desert. It's also a great whaling centre, if that's your thing!

***Edward Bohlen*** *ship on Skeleton Coast, Namibia*

I chose the trip to Swakopmund, about 30km up the coast, and found it a fascinating hangover from the days of German South West Africa before 1945. It's like a piece of Bavaria transplanted to Africa! The Lutheran Church, the Bezirksgericht, a former legal building now a holiday home for Namibia's President, Alte Kaserne, the Woermann House, now the Public Library, the Hohernzollern House and the former railway station, now an hotel, are all thoroughly Germanic! And the local sewage farm is a paradise for bird watchers! They call it the 'Bird Paradise!' Out to sea there's Bird Island - a huge wooden platform built to provide roosting and nesting space for seabirds. And we were told it also produces 1,000 tons of bird guano annually! Seals and dolphins are also seen on coastal cruises.

I couldn't go on the 'Eco Dune Adventure' into the Namibian desert as well as visiting Swakopmund, but guests who did go told me I'd really missed something. It's the world's oldest desert and it's a striking scorched-red colour. As the sand is constantly shifting, skillful drivers are necessary to see the wild life- hyenas, jackals, snakes and reptiles like the chameleon thrive in the desert, along with ostriches and baboons. I had to content myself with views of the desert as we sailed on for two more days towards Cape Town, passing en route the extraordinary sight of the *Edward Bohlen,* a German cargo ship that ran aground back in 1907, while it was on its way to Table Bay from Swakopmund. Thick fog caused the ship to founder close to Conception Bay. Then the desert began to encroach on the ocean and the ship that was once stranded in the ocean slowly became stranded in the desert. The wreck is currently about 500 metres from the ocean. Space does not permit us to investigate the other 999 such wrecks along the 'Skeleton Coast!' But *Saga Ruby* survived!

Our arrival in Cape Town was as impressive as I'd been led to believe it would be. Table Mountain forms the background to the city and across the top were the clouds, falling down the sides of the mountain just like a tablecloth! We docked in front of Table Mountain and I remembered the stories of the 'Lady in White' who used to come down to the pier to welcome and wave off all the liners. There was no sign of her - no doubt she had passed on to the great port in the heavens! What there *was* awaiting us was a whole posse of passport officials! They boarded the *Ruby* and took up positions at tables set up in the lounge. Then we all had to queue up to get our passports stamped and our Temporary Residence permits. They certainly made a meal of it, as so often in developing countries. Of course, it provides much-needed work, so one has to bear it all patiently.

*Approaching Cape Town and Table Mountain with its 'cloth'*

When I finally was able to disembark I noticed a group of grey seals lazily swimming just in front of the *Ruby* and then basking on the quayside. But nobody fed them, to their dismay, no doubt! As in so many old ports, many of the former dock buildings have been converted into shopping malls, a new hotel and so on. The revitalized area's called the 'Victoria and *Alfred* Waterfront.' N.B. *not* 'Albert!' Alfred was Victoria's second son. But locals just call it, 'The Waterfront.'

The city itself is open and pleasant and I felt quite safe exploring its landmarks by myself. The Anglican cathedral, like the one in Gibraltar, is a reminder of old-style colonial Britain, with its memorials to soldiers and ex-patriots. The Groote Kerk is the most important Dutch Reformed church and the oldest in Cape Town, dating back to 1704. Inside there's a huge Baroque-style pulpit dating from 1789. It's one of Cape Town's most treasured works and it certainly brings out the Reformed Church's insistence on the primacy of The Word in their worship!

The Old Slave Lodge has less happy associations, having been used to shelter slaves brought to the Cape by the Dutch East India Company. It's the second oldest building in Cape Town, after the Castle of Good Hope itself. Now it's a Cultural History Museum. When I visited it there was still an eclectic collection of objects on display- some important Greek vases, exhibits covering early Cape history, especially artefacts of the Khoisan herders, and 'postal stones.' These were used to shelter messages left under them by homesick mariners, hoping fellow travellers would deliver them home for them. I found them very moving. But the plan was to change the place into an Anti-Slavery Museum!

My favourite visit was to the Kirstenbosch National Botanical Garden. It's on the lower slopes of Table Mountain, on land bequeathed to the Nation by Cecil Rhodes. His magnificent memorial is close by. It was designed by Sir Herbert Baker, with a typically grand flight of 49 steps - one for each year of Rhodes' life - leading up to an equestrian statue. Baker was a dominant force in South African architecture for two decades, and also a major designer of some of New Delhi's most notable government buildings.

On 18 September 2015, the bronze bust of Rhodes at the memorial was vandalised. The nose was cut off and the memorial was daubed with graffiti accusing Rhodes of being a "Racist, thief, [and] murderer." It appeared that the vandals had attempted to cut off the whole head. This was the work of the 'Rhodes Must Fall' movement, which also attempted to get his statue removed from the façade of Oriel College

Oxford. The college was about to comply with their demands, until they suffered a huge reduction in old members' donations and reversed their decision!

You drive out to the Garden through a very exclusive residential area, with large houses, one of which was the Archbishop of Cape Town, Desmond Tutu's residence. There are magnificent views up towards Table Mountain and the park has a wonderfully colourful variety of mostly indigenous plants, over 5000 species spread over 560 hectares and set among streams and dells. The Cape Agapanthi were as beautiful as they were in Madeira and the Cape snowdrops flowered prolifically in the valleys and dells, just like the famous displays at Colesbourne Park in Gloucestershire. In contrast, the bright red salvia took me back to our old garden at home.

I could have stayed all day, but I wanted to get on to explore Table Mountain itself. You have to wait until the weather's clear and not too windy for the cable car that takes you up to the top to be operating, but I was lucky. The cable car rotates as it ascends, which gives everyone thrilling all-round views. There's a tremendous feeling of space when you get up to the top, with a magnificent panorama stretching away to the Lion's Head, which really does have the same outline as one of the lions at the base of Nelson's Column in Trafalgar Square.

*The Rhodes Memorial, Cape Town*

On the ship's final evening in Cape Town a special concert was laid on by Saga for us all in Cape Town's City Hall to mark the 60<sup>th</sup> anniversary of the Commonwealth. We were all to have an early dinner aboard and then coaches would take us to the venue. When we got to the coaches, all lined up at the harbour, we were each given a 'paddle' sign to hold up and marshal our group. I was very amused to see Lord Steel, the former Liberal Party Leader and a fellow lecturer on board, in charge of the coach next door gamely holding up his 'paddle!' At least we weren't called on to distribute the ubiquitous Wernher toffees that Saga usually insists on the escort taking round the coach on excursions!

The City Hall proved to be a very grand Edwardian-style building, but it had no air conditioning and we had all dressed up for the gala evening! Saga had rolled out the red carpet and flown out Lesley Garrett, the opera singer and broadcaster, especially to sing to us. She made a dramatic appearance in a wonderful red, white and blue creation. The programme varied from 'crossover' songs like *When I Fall in*

*Love* to *Amazing Grace* and ended with a rousing rendition of *Rule Britannia* in which we all joined, waving the Union Jacks that Saga had thoughtfully provided! I couldn't help but wonder how appropriate all that was in the 'Rainbow Nation's' main city!

Next day I left *Saga Ruby* before she sailed on to Durban and then back home via Suez. I wanted to explore a little more by myself, before I flew home in three days' time. In the afternoon I visited the 'Nellie' - the grand old colonial style Mount Nelson Hotel in the city centre - for a sumptuous tea and a swim in its lovely gardens. I rather wished I'd splashed out on staying there! I'm not sure if swimming was really available to non-residents, but I just found a little place in which to change and then plunged in! I made a vow to return and stay in the Nellie, but I read recently that guests staying there had been held up at gunpoint by intruders who demanded their cash, valuables and watches! So perhaps I was safer where I was!

From my B & B in Sea Point I made another trip along the coast through some very upmarket resorts like Camp's Bay, backed by the magnificent Twelve Apostles mountain range behind. There's a lovely sea-water pool there, with rather primitive public changing facilities, but wonderfully bracing swimming! The sea itself would have been even colder, and swimming in it would have been almost impossible, due to the huge sea weed clusters- to say nothing of any lurking sharks!

Later I went into town to take the train down to Simonstown, the former Royal Naval base further South down the coast. I remembered there had been something called the 'Simonstown Agreement' which gave the Royal Navy rights to continue to use the base there, after it had been handed over to the South African Navy. That caused shock and horror in liberal circles! Simonstown itself was a small, old–fashioned settlement, which reminded me a bit of Gibraltar before it smartened itself up. One of the attractions there is the flocks of penguins, who were happily waddling along the shore. I had been warned only to travel in First Class on the train, but it seemed to me that people boarding paid little attention to this and there were no inspectors! One was, in fact, probably more vulnerable to robbery in the First Class section, but all was well.

Next day I had booked myself on a full day tour of the winelands. The minibus, with a pleasant young man as our driver-guide, picked me up from my B & B early and we drove out to Stellenbosch, a very attractive university town in the Western Cape province. The Cape Dutch architecture echoes Dutch buildings back in the Netherlands, but on a smaller scale. There's also much more vegetation around than in the Netherlands: streets were lined with oak and other trees and the vineyards of the Cape Winelands surrounded the town. In the distance were the mountainous nature reserves of Jonkershoek and Simonsberg. There were many cafes, boutiques and art galleries. Lunch was included in a delightful wine lodge, up amongst the vines growing all around. The seared scallops paired with a delicious Chenin Blanc were my favourite. South African food has made enormous strides since the days of Empire and there are many innovative chefs working with excellent materials. Likewise, South African wine can now compete with any of the best wine areas of the world, as our tasting of both white and red varieties confirmed. I only wished it was practical to take a pack back with me, but sadly air travel makes that impractical.

My final trip was the 30 minute boat trip out from the harbour to rocky Robben Island, the former prison where Nelson Mandela was held for 18 of the 27 years he spent in prison, until President F.W. de Klerk released him in 1990. I was struck by the bleak rocky landscape and the bare stone buildings. It was sobering to stand in Mandela's stark former cell and think what 18 years there must have been like. The island takes its name from the Dutch word for 'seal', like those in Cape Town harbour. I found my visit made me appreciate even more the way in which Mandela was able to triumph over adversity and forgive his former captors when he took over a President of the Republic in 1994. I'm sorry to say that his successors been unable to live up to his legacy.

*Mandela's former cell on Robben Island*

On my last morning I switched on the television to find that the UK had experienced heavy snowfalls and Heathrow Airport was closed! I tried to check in on line and found the flight showing as cancelled! What to do, with my room booked by another guest from midday? Eventually, I decided the best thing was to get to the airport and sit it out there until a flight was available. The road to Cape Town's airport takes you past huge areas of shanties. I reflected that the cheerful staff who had looked after one so well in the guest house and at the 'Nellie' probably lived in places like that. It put the inconvenience of hanging around for some hours at the airport into some perspective!

Talking of staff, in the old days one was always expected on the night before departure to tip one's cabin steward and table steward at least, plus anyone else who had been especially helpful. Bar staff used to be rewarded directly in cash when one paid for drinks, in the days before cashless ships came in. Nowadays many cruise lines simply add an amount to one's final bill, but the 'ultra luxury' lines like Seabourn, Silversea, Crystal and Regent, advertise that tipping is no longer expected or required on board their ships, since personnel are presumably compensated in their pay levels. Saga also advertise that all tipping is included on board their ships. However, it seems a number of Saga's guests like to add a personal tip as well. There's nothing wrong with this, of course. Some passengers become very fond of crew members. But it seemed to have got rather out of control some years ago, when I noticed an envelope had been prominently placed on my suitcase by my cabin steward! I moved it, but it returned! Eventually I felt obliged to put a note in it. When I returned home I checked with Saga's office and was told that tips were quite definitely already included.

On my next voyage in the *Ruby* I experienced the usual difficulty in the Dining Room. As a lecturer one is expected to wait to see if there are any free places, since guests, of course, must come first. Eventually, the Head Waiter showed me, along with my friend the film lecturer and his guest, to a free table near the entrance to the galley. No